The Three Fears Every Leader Has to Know

"With this seminal work, Norheim and Haga opens a new chapter in their ongoing reflection on rhetoric and leadership. They argue that an adequate appeal to fear is decisive for a leader who wants to appear credible during a crisis. They describe and explore three kinds of fears – apocalyptic fear, political fear, and private fear. The book is directed at any leader and speaker who wants to reflect on the art of speaking well when things are not going so well. They further offer tools for self-reflection, motifs for critical analysis, and gives advice and guidelines on how to craft a powerful and effective address when a minor or major crisis is emerging, as we all experienced during the Covid-19 pandemic. This book will enrich not only academics and church leaders and students, but all who are interested in the dynamics of words to use in a crisis."

—Ian Nell, *Stellenbosch University, South Africa*

"This book has become even more important by the war and suffering that is currently unfolding before our very eyes in the heart of Europe. It is exactly at times of crisis and war, leaders need to be heard and understood, as well as offer powerful words of inspiration and action. "If people experience a crisis, the speaker need to name that reality," the two authors rightly emphasis in this important book. Few have done it better than the Ukrainian President Volodymyr Zelensky. In the midst of war, suffering and anxiety, his speeches have been truly inspiring. No-one can stay indifferent when President Zelensky speaks, as he quickly rattles any trace of complacency immediately out of his audience. And through a series of cleverly tailored messages, he has also in a very short period of time been able to muster extraordinary and widespread international support. His unconventional, direct rhetoric is also what this book helps us better understand, while at the same time giving us advice and concrete guidelines on how to craft a powerful and effective address, when a minor or major crisis is emerging."

—Bjørn Berge, *Deputy Secretary General in the Council of Europe*

Bård Norheim · Joar Haga

The Three Fears Every Leader Has to Know

Words to Use in a Crisis

Bård Norheim
NLA University College
Bergen, Norway

Joar Haga
NLA University College
Bergen, Norway

ISBN 978-3-031-08983-1   ISBN 978-3-031-08984-8   (eBook)
https://doi.org/10.1007/978-3-031-08984-8

Cover credit: © Harvey Loake

This Palgrave Macmillan imprint is published by the registered company Springer Nature Switzerland AG
The registered company address is: Gewerbestrasse 11, 6330 Cham, Switzerland

PREFACE

Shortly after Joe Biden's inauguration as US President in January 2021, more than 150 influential world leaders sent an open letter to the new President to pledge their support to his vision to combat climate change. The letter was supportive, but it also appealed to fear. The signatories exhorted Biden to lead humanity away from "the cliff's edge":

> You can be remembered as the "climate president" who led humanity away from the cliff's edge. You can transform the world's energy systems from fossil fuels to clean energy, while also creating an abundance of jobs, reducing harmful pollution, and tackling economic, racial, and health inequality in the process.[1]

The metaphor "the cliff's edge" indicates that the world is at a point where it may collapse. At a cliff's edge, we are threatened by extinction and death, literally hanging by the tip of our fingernails to avoid falling into the dark abyss. Therefore, people like Amazon boss Jeff Bezos argued that the current decade is "the most decisive decade in human history to confront the climate crisis." Unlike, most motivational speeches and inspirational quotes, these leaders used fear to give an adequate account

---

[1] Open letter to Joe Biden from 150 world leaders: https://climatepower.us/world-leaders/.

of reality. Given the major challenges ahead, fear is not an illusion, so was the message.

Most of us appeal to fear on many occasions, typically when we sense a threat or a crisis. This book discusses the appeal to fear and what aims it may serve. The purpose of the book is to help leaders identify the fears at play at a certain time and a certain place, and how to speak to that fear in an adequate and perhaps even constructive manner. The book is a study in rhetoric and leadership, arguing that an adequate appeal to fear is decisive for a leader who wants to appear credible during a crisis. Rhetoric concerns the art of persuasion. It gives an assessment of what it means to speak convincingly. In the book we describe and explore three kinds of fears—apocalyptic fear, political fear, and private fear. The focus is set on the leader who needs to communicate when a crisis strikes, and fear is imminent. The book is therefore directed at any leader and speaker who wants to reflect on the art of speaking well when things are not going so well, whether in politics, sports, business, NGO work, civil or community service, or elsewhere. The book builds on insights from our previous book on rhetoric and leadership, *The Four Speeches Every Leader Has to Know* (2020), where we focused on what it takes for leaders to motivate followers, even in times of hardship and suffering. In that book we argued that there are four speeches every leader needs to know—the opening speech, the executioner speech, the consolation speech, and the farewell speech.[2]

In this book on the three fears, we offer tools for self-reflection, motifs for critical analysis, and give advice and guidelines on how to craft a powerful and effective address when a minor or major crisis is emerging. Simultaneously, the book also offers an interpretative framework for those who want to reflect on the ongoing energy and climate crisis. What role should the appeal to fear have as we try to address the challenges of global warming? In the first chapter of the book, we discuss the appeal to fear in the light of various conceptions of fear throughout history. We also consider what may characterize bad, or ineffective uses of fear. In the second chapter, we present the reader with two different stories. First, we tell the story of the three kinds of fear, and how they relate to three different places—nature, culture, and the place we call home. Secondly,

---

[2] Norheim, Bård and Haga, Joar: *The Four Speeches. Every Leader Has to Know.* London: Palgrave Macmillan (Palgrave Pivot), 2020.

we contrast the story of the three fears with the history of the ongoing energy crisis and how it has shaped and still shapes our feeling of fear in multiple ways.

In Chapter 3 we examine *apocalyptic* fear more in-depth. Here we have the most dramatic fear in mind, the sort of fear that appears to threaten our very existence. It is the fear that nature may be collapsing, and that the world is coming to an end. We therefore label this type of fear first-level fear, or *T0*. In Chapter 4, we explore political fear. It is the fear that our society or culture may be at risk. This sort of fear reminds us that our shared rules, rituals, and regulations might be threatened. We label this second-level fear, or *T1*. In Chapter 5 we deal with a third type of fear, which is the kind of fear that threatens the place we call home or our house. It may include the fear of losing your job, your family, your actual house, or even losing your sense of being your true self. This is the feeling that your authentic, autonomous, and perhaps even moral way of living, may be at risk. We call this sort of fear *private* fear, and label it third-level fear, or *T2*.

In Chapter 6 we examine how the speaker should dress up to address all the three kinds of fear. We discuss how the leader should use and develop her rhetorical wardrobe to appeal to fear in an adequate and credible manner. Exploring what kind of words, metaphors, gestures, and styles of the speech the leader should make use of, we argue that the speaker's rhetorical bandwidth may be expanded by practice. Here we emphasize the importance of the character the speaker takes on and the diligent and wisely calibrated use of genre when you aim to appeal to fear in a well-founded and convincing manner. In the final chapter, we ask how the appeal to fear may serve as an appeal to act virtuously in the face of crisis. Throughout the book, we draw on classical rhetorical theory, leadership studies, philosophy, sociology, theology, psychology, and insights from other sciences to argue how a leader may appeal to the three fears by using tools, skills, means, and modes to appear persuasive and credible.

So, why focus on fear? Basically, because fear is an inescapable part of how human beings experience reality. Every leader faced with a crisis, therefore, needs to ask: How should I address fear to offer a well-founded and effective response to the challenge at hand?

NOTE TO THE READER

The writing of the manuscript was finished before Russia invaded Ukraine on February 24, 2022. Although we were not able to analyze and discuss the speeches given during the outbreak of the war in any comprehensive manner, the war has displayed the effect of appealing to fear in adequate and less adequate manners.

Bergen, Norway   Bård Norheim
Stavanger, Norway   Joar Haga
May 2022

ACKNOWLEDGEMENTS

First, we are grateful to our editor Ambra Finotello and Palgrave Macmillan for their efforts to get this book published. We would also like to express our gratitude to Andrew Root, Graham Stanton, and Dion Forster for inspiring conversations on rhetoric and leadership in our podcast series *The Four Speeches*. Similarly, we are thankful to Torgeir von Essen for reading the manuscript and offering many helpful comments. Big thanks to Timothy Meadors for proofreading. And finally, thanks to Kjersti Gautestad Norheim and Britt Marit Haga for reading the manuscript and inducing a sufficient amount of constructive, "domestic fear" for us to finish the book.

CONTENTS

CHAPTER 1

The Dilemma of Fear

Abstract The first chapter of the book discusses the appeal to fear in the light of various conceptions of fear throughout history. We examine how thinkers like Aristotle, Augustine, Macchiavelli, Rousseau, Darwin, and Freud interpret the role of fear in the lives of human beings, and how contemporary voices like Martha Nussbaum, Zygmunt Bauman, Elemèr Hankiss, and Nassim Nicholas Taleb explore the paradox of fear and human beings' response to the arrival of a crisis. We also investigate the appeal to fear as a rhetorical dilemma. The chapter offers an introduction to the art of appealing to fear and how to calibrate that appeal by relating to where people are at.

Keywords Fear · Crisis · Utopia · Dystopia · The paradox of fear · Existential fear · Hierarchies of fear · Fear as a moral and rhetorical dilemma

AN EPILOGUE FOR THE CAR

Just before Christmas 1973 the two authors of this book were toddlers and approximately six months old. If our parents would have wanted to take us on a car ride on a cold Sunday through Norwegian winter wonderland, they would be in big trouble. Due to the international oil

B. Norheim and J. Haga, *The Three Fears Every Leader Has to Know*, https://doi.org/10.1007/978-3-031-08984-8_1

crisis, which followed the Yom Kippur War in October 1973, the Norwegian government banned the use of cars on Sundays to secure the supply of gas. As a result of the ban, the streets were all empty. Some people started to go skiing in the streets. Even the Norwegian monarch, King Olav V, gave his driver a day off and took the metro to get around the capital city of Oslo. 50 years later things have changed dramatically. If you drive a car, you're not necessarily in trouble, but people might give you a condescending look, particularly if your car is not considered to be environmentally friendly, or if the ride itself is considered to be unnecessary. Some cities in Norway, and many other cities around Europe, want to ban the use of diesel cars.

The car, the *automobile*, is a symbol of freedom. The freedom to move is possibly the most poignant expression of our search for freedom. A driver conquers the world with his car, as he drives through an isolated desert, cruises on an endless highway, or passes through the deserted streets of an inner-city at night. Even your choice of car is taken to be a statement of who you are. If you drive a Volvo, you're obsessed with safety. If you drive a Ferrari, you're obsessed with yourself. Human beings express themselves through personal choice, and choosing the right car is not a mere display of reason at work, unless you buy a Toyota or a Ford.

The car is also a symbol of security. A car is meant to give you a feeling of protection and keep you safe from fears. After all, where would you want to be when lightning strikes and nature unleashes its unpredictable forces? On the other hand, the car has become the symbol of all that is wrong with the world. For some, the extensive use of cars reminds them of the possibility of human extinction, as the use of fossil fuel contributes to global warming.

This book is not about cars, but fear, and how leaders should appeal to fear. The book tells two stories simultaneously. The first is a story about three kinds of fear, and how a leader may give an adequate appeal to fear during a crisis. The second story is a story of an ongoing crisis, the oil crisis. In October 1973 the international oil crisis exploded with the outbreak of the Yom Kippur War. The war was a conflict between several Arab countries, headed by Egypt and Syria, and Israel. As a response to US support for Israel, the Arab members of *OPEC*, The Organization of Petroleum Exporting Countries, spearheaded by Saudi Arabia, decided to reduce its oil production. After US President Nixon authorized the use of arms supplies and promised economic support for Israel two days later, Saudi Arabia declared an oil embargo against the United States. Later, other oil exporters joined and extended the embargo to the Netherlands and many other states. As a result, restrictions on the use of gasoline were installed in many countries around the world, like Norway.

Why focus on fear? Isn't the appeal to fear an obstacle for a leader who wants to motivate followers? 40 years before the oil crisis following the Yom Kippur War in 1973, the newly elected American president Franklin Delano Roosevelt, FDR, gave his inaugural address, on March 4, 1933. FDR was addressing a nation during The Great Depression. At the beginning of his speech the President proclaimed that:

> The only thing we have to fear is fear itself – nameless, unreasoning, unjustified terror which paralyzes needed efforts to convert retreat into advance.

At first glance, FDR's appeal to the American people seems like an echo of all the world's motivational speeches. They tell you to dream big and never be afraid, as FDR continued:

> To stop at nothing to overcome your fears.
> To embrace failure and be courageous.[1]

Was FDR right in claiming that the only fear to fear is fear itself? Is fear an illusion that human beings should conquer with the use of sophisticated mind games?

Consider former British Prime Minister, Neville Chamberlain, who on September 30, 1938, gave a speech outside Downing Street 10 in London. He delivered a defence for the newly signed Munich Peace Agreement with German Chancellor Adolf Hitler. In the speech Chamberlain famously proclaimed that "I believe it is peace for our time."[2] In the Munich agreement, Sudetenland was assigned from Czechoslovakia to Germany without any Czechoslovakian involvement in the negotiations. The agreement strengthened the German military position and showed to have little value when Germany invaded Poland less than a year later and marked the start of the second world war. Chamberlain has been harshly judged for his failure to address the threat of an aggressive Nazi Germany. In hindsight, the British Prime Minister should have evaluated the situation differently and appealed to the fear of Hitler's rule.

THE APPEAL TO FEAR

We often hear that a leader should avoid any appeal to fear. Appealing to fear is supposed to be morally dubious. However, when the going gets tough, an appeal to fear may be necessary and expected. If people experience a crisis, the speaker needs to name that reality. Appealing to fear may serve a constructive purpose if the appeal gives an adequate account of reality. On closer look, FDR's attack on the paralyzing psychological effect of the Great Depression in 1933 was not an appeal to ignore fear. It was rather an attempt to address the imminent experience of fear. In his speech, FDR used fear to form a persuasive argument for collective efforts, like the nationwide highway expansion program.

Similarly, no one questions a parent shouting out to one of their kids, "Hey, Martin! Watch out for the traffic!" If young Martin is about to run off into heavy Friday rush hour traffic, it would appear rather irresponsible, if his parents would fail to warn him. Faced with a crisis, most leaders appeal to fear. More importantly, we, the people, expect our leaders to do so.

The feeling of fear is a fundamental human experience. However, claiming that an appeal to fear might be justified, seems to open the door to irrationality. Does the appeal to fear put the speaker in the position of the demagogue? A demagogue is a political leader who exploits an issue or a situation by appealing to the popular desires and prejudices of ordinary people. However, this book is not a handbook in demagogic rhetoric. Rather, the book wants to explore constructive ways to use fear when communicating in a crisis. We even want to examine the rational arguments for doing so.

Let us now return to young Martin, who is running head over heels into heavy traffic: What if Martin's parents are faced with the following dilemma: Just as they are about to shout out to Martin, they spot Martin's kindergarten teacher, Chelsea, and are reminded of the last parent–teacher consultation. Here Chelsea admonished Martin's parents to be less vocal in bringing up their son. "You simply need to shout less!" Martin's dad, Steve, vividly remembers Chelsea's sharp tone, fearing that she would most likely contact a child protection officer at the city's social services, if they would fail to adhere to Chelsea's moral reminder. Most parents would have no problem prioritizing between the two fears at play here, and still shout out from the top of their lungs. After all, one fear, the fear that their son's life may be in danger, easily triumphs the other.

Let us consider a different dilemma. The mayor of a city, Susan McKnowsaum, is summoned to an emergency meeting with her brand-new task force, which specializes in risk identification, risk analysis, and risk evaluation. At the meeting, she receives information that there is a 10% chance the town will be hit by a giant meteor within the hour. What should the mayor do? If the meteor hits the city, the whole place will most probably be annihilated.

As the mayor is about to call her media team to set up an emergency press conference, she asks herself: What if the meteor misses, or never reaches earth at all? If she strikes the apocalyptic chord in vain, how on earth will she be able to shrug off all the negative media attention afterwards? One thing is that her upcoming re-election will go down the drain, but another fear appears even more prominent: A failed appeal to fear will most likely lead to more riots and protests in the suburbs and the poorer areas in the north-eastern parts of the city. After the lockdown and restrictions following the pandemic a few years back, most people have grown sceptical of any politician who uses the word "crisis." And even worse, in some areas people seem to easily turn against their neighbours. The mayor misses the feeling of solidarity in the good old days. "Argh, this is not an easy call! These last few years it feels like the whole community is constantly on the brink of a sort of civil war, a cultural collapse," she mourns to her press officer. "Well, you're damned if you do, and damned if you don't, right?" is the phlegmatic response that escapes the lips of the officer.

Then another member of the task force approaches the mayor, saying that they have received new information. New estimates indicate that the meteor will hit the outskirts of the city. The task force cannot be 100% sure, but most likely only minor parts of the city will be destroyed. The mayor looks at the map which fixates the estimated strike point. She immediately realizes that it is right where her only daughter goes to school. The mayor suddenly finds herself captured with a paralysing fear, more personal in a sense. What should she do? What fears should be prioritized as she considers how to address the townspeople? Very few of us will ever find ourselves in a situation as extreme and difficult as the mayor of this city, but many of us will have to consider which fears to prioritize when the going gets tough.

Words for a Crisis

Leaders face these dilemmas all the time. We call it a *crisis*. A crisis means the arrival of one or more threats that challenge the way we think, act and structure our lives. A crisis calls for leadership, and a leader needs to give an adequate and persuasive account of reality. The leader must be able to understand what's going on and perhaps propose a way forward to cope with the crisis. In a crisis sound judgement is critical. We expect a wise leader to be able to exercise his *judicium*, to discern well.

A crisis simultaneously presents us with the dilemma of fear. What is the best way, and perhaps even the right way, to appeal to fear when a crisis strikes? The leader's dilemma is which fear to prioritize as she addresses her audience. She needs to consider carefully what sort of response the situation calls for, and then try to calibrate a well-articulated and fitting speech. A crisis reminds the speaker and her listeners that there is something to pay special attention to, possibly something to be afraid of. As a real crisis evolves, we may fear that the situation could turn into a disaster, and the public, therefore, expects urgent and vigorous action. They expect someone to take leadership by naming reality and setting a course. This is equally true if you are a leader of a state facing a national emergency or a CEO facing company bankruptcy.

In a crisis, the use of words is of great importance. Rhetoric deals with the art of persuading an audience using words and other means of communication. When a crisis strikes, we expect a leader to give a credible and convincing account of the current reality and, based on that account, propose a way forward. In other words, when a leader says "crisis," the audience expects a persuasive call to action. The word "crisis" usually opens an avenue of ample opportunities to call an audience to action.

Let's say you attend the general assembly of the local sports club. Having heard the annual report of the chairman, which describes a steep decline in the number of volunteers, the guy next to you shouts out, "Come on, guys, we can't pretend this is business as usual! Unless we do something, there will be no sports practice for our kids after the summer holidays!" Suddenly, the failure to recruit new volunteer leaders to the local sports club, becomes an opportunity to launch a wide-range critique of how the club is run and perhaps propose a reform. Pulling the "crisis"-button creates room for persuasion and passionate appeals. Or let us consider the following example: If you suggest that the upcoming election is about to become a potential disaster for a given political party, someone could use the perceived crisis as a pretext to overthrow the current leadership.

When someone uses the word "crisis," it forces us to clarify the pros and cons. Calling something a crisis, helps legitimize decisions. Consider the following two examples: If the sheriff of a crime-ridden town calls the current police department budgeting an accident waiting to happen, people will probably listen more carefully as he suggests drastic measures. If the school headmaster calls the parents' failure to support their kids in their learning endeavours a betrayal, he may use that accusation to legitimize his proposal to install compulsory "homework" sessions at school with school tutors.

Originally the word "crisis" stems from the Greek *krisis*, which points to the division of two opposites. In antiquity a *"krisis"* demanded clear alternatives: What is right or wrong? Does the suggested path of action lead to salvation or condemnation, life or death? This sharp notion of a crisis was later, from the seventeenth century and onwards, supplemented with a more metaphorical interpretation, which expanded the meaning of the word "crisis." The word crisis now designated both the objective, the crisis itself, and the potential critique, the subjective.

It comes as no surprise, then, that Aristotle underlined that a *krisis* is something that affects the order of a civic community.[3] A crisis required sound judgement or discernment—what the Romans called *judicium*. In 1762 Jean-Jacques Rousseau wrote *The Social Contract*, a cornerstone in political and social theory. Here Rousseau used the term "crisis" to point to a possible future revolution. His understanding of a crisis was based on his account of the current reality, where he criticized the contemporary culture and the idealization of that culture.[4]

The term "crisis" points to the future. If we articulate the word "crisis," we evoke ideas of what the future may hold. Do we envision a future Utopia, that ignites our fight for change? Or do we fear the imminent emergence of a Dystopia? Anyhow, our vision of the future serves as a prism through which we calibrate our call to action. We also need to distinguish between two kinds of crises. First, some crises are not repeatable, like the destruction of the planet and humankind through a nuclear war. Secondly, other crises represent repeatable phenomena, like a pandemic. The latter could be cured by a vaccine, but possibly return later in another form. The crucial point in this book is that a crisis, and the fears that may follow, fixates the importance of rhetoric. As we have already pointed out, rhetoric deals with the art of persuasion, and in a crisis taking leadership means speaking out to argue why one course of action is more justified or desirable than others.

In a crisis, leaders, like parents, want to persuade their followers to make the best possible choice. The leader invites the audience to consider the pros and cons and exercise sound judgement. Sometimes this implies choosing the lesser of two evils. Another key element in a rhetorical approach to a crisis is identifying who earns the right to set a diagnosis of the ongoing crisis. Who seizes the word and names reality when a crisis strikes?

Fundamentally, a crisis reminds us, that something is at stake. You could miss out on a life-changing opportunity, and lose your job or your health. You could increase or lose your social status, even your very existence might be threatened. When something's at stake, in any situation that offers alternatives, fear is always an option. It could be the paralysing fear that the whole world may be coming to an end. Or the fear that our culture or political system is at risk. It could even be the fear of failure or the fear of missing out. The list goes on.

What passes as a trustworthy account of reality? In a political sense, the problem may be phrased in the following manner: Do you trust your neighbour? Most people would probably claim that they trust their neighbour but usually only to a certain point. We still build fences or check that our kids have arrived home safely. In other words, empirically trust is not the only category by which we order our lives. We learn that it may be wise to trust our neighbour, but it may also be wise to stick to a realistic perception of the world. The world, as we know it, is not a perfect place, and there are things around that it might be wise to fear. Our point in this book is that in a given situation an appeal to fear may be well-founded and even serve a constructive purpose.

A Short History of Fear

The feeling of fear seems to be an inevitable part of the human condition. The Roman poet *Statius* argued that fear was the first creation of the gods. In the Bible, in Proverbs 9 verse 10, we read about how fear of God is the beginning of Wisdom. We may react differently to the feeling of fear that an emerging threat represents. The fight-flight-freeze response is known as the human body's natural reaction to danger. Perhaps we might even rehearse and tweak our response to felt fear, but the point here is the following: fear is.

Aristotle pointed out that the intended effect of seeing someone suffer is to feel sorry for them, and then to fear as a result. Aristotle also differentiated between fear and anxiety. Fear demands an object. Anxiety on the other hand requires no object. This implies that fear needs to relate to something in our immediate proximity for it to take real hold of us. Aristotle, therefore, suggested that the most impressive stories are complex plots that give rise to both fear and pity, as fear holds the capacity to cleanse the mind and the whole being of an audience through what the Greeks called "*catharsis*"—purification.[5]

To Aristotle fear is caused by something that we think holds the power to destroy us, or even harm us in ways that tend to cause us great pain. But since human beings master language, we can use the feeling of fear and the appeal to that feeling for our own purposes. The problem is that the feeling of fear unleashes the irrational and creates a sense of suspicion to both language and feelings. In other words, we learn from the feeling of fear that our senses may fool us. Church Father Saint Augustine argued that fear regards good as its proper object. Drawing on the Apostle Paul, Augustine underlines that the fear-instigating powers of earthly authorities have their proper purpose. The point is to restrain human sinfulness by the appeal to worldly fear. Therefore, the wise ruler of an earthly city should acknowledge and try to manage the public's fears of want, slavery, and death. However, for Augustine the reach of this worldly fear is limited. It is a spiritual dead-end, as you cannot organize your life around worldly loyalties and loves. Another problem is the fact that the fear of suffering and death may all too easily be an effective tool for the malicious plans of demagogues and tyrants. Even if we consider the fruits from a more pragmatic perspective, Augustine found that the kind of justice that may emerge out of trembling anxiety and fear is something outward and unstable.[6]

Nicolo Machiavelli is often considered the father of modern political philosophy and political science. In 1513 he wrote *The Prince* as a set of advice to a ruler who wants to keep control of a city or a nation. In the essay, he drew on his own experience as secretary to the Second Chancery of the Republic of Florence from 1498 to 1512, when the house of Medici was not in power. Machiavelli was not so interested in philosophical and theological reflections on the object of fear; rather, he was more interested in the use of fear in what we would now call political communication. If the leader must make a choice between appealing to fear or love, he should choose fear, Machiavelli found. The problem is that it is difficult to combine them. It is, therefore, far better to be feared than loved if you cannot be both, Machiavelli claimed. In other words, ruling by fear is considered more effective than ruling by love.[7] Acknowledging that appealing to fear is more effective than appealing to love, marks the birth of modern politics.

THE PARADOX OF FEAR

We live with a relative absence of fear in our everyday lives. With the creation of modern civilization, nature is no longer per se a danger zone to humans. Human beings have managed to develop belief systems, behavioural patterns, and institutions, which seem to protect us from external fears. But this is just the first part of the story of fear: Existential fear is still a generative force in the development of human civilization. The success of human beings or human progression rests on mankind's ability to tame raw and destructive fear and use that fear to build civilizations. A civilization, with its symbolic structures, aims to protect people against the danger of the outer, alien world and the fears and anxieties of the inner world, the hearts, and minds of people. Sociologist Elemér Hankiss described the paradox of fear. He found that on one hand, human beings seem to master fear, as fear seems to play a less prominent role in the life of human beings than in the life of animals. On the other hand, *homo sapiens* seem more fear-ridden than any other species on earth.[8]

The 90s' hit song will tell us that *love is all around*, but sociologist Zygmunt Bauman has argued that it is more telling to claim that *fear is all around*. Bauman spoke of the "ubiquity of fear." Fear is like liquid. It may leak out of any place, situation, encounter, or part of nature. He also distinguished between different kinds of fear, where first degree-fear is an experience common to all animals.[9] This resembles Charles Darwin's point in *On the Origin of Species* that no fear is felt in the struggle for existence and survival in nature. In the struggle to survive, or the "war of nature" as Darwin called it, fear is not incessant, as death generally arrives promptly. On the flip side the vigorous, the healthy, and the happy survive and multiply.[10]

Second degree-fear, on the other hand, is a fear that is socially or culturally recycled and thus, guides the behaviour of human beings. It is a feeling of vulnerability, of being susceptible to danger. Human beings are, in some sense, charged with fear, Bauman maintained. He, therefore, suggested that there are three kinds of dangers:

1. Dangers threatening the body and possessions
2. Dangers threatening the reliability and durability of the social order
3. Dangers threatening a person's place in the world—a position in the social hierarchy, identity.

Based on these elaborations, Bauman described what he calls the "Titanic syndrome." According to traditional leadership theory, the "Titanic Syndrome" usually recounts a corporate disease, where organizations facing disruption and change bring about their own ruin through arrogance, excessive reliance, and attachment to a successful past, or a failure to recognize the challenges of a new and emerging reality.[11] Bauman's definition of the "Titanic Syndrome" is more existential. To him, it designates the horror of falling through the "wafer-thin crust" of civilization into a sort of nothingness stripped of the usual, elementary staples of organized, civilized life, that we think we know so well. Fears emanating from what Bauman called the "Titanic syndrome" is the fear that a catastrophe may descend on us all, hitting us blindly and indiscriminately, even randomly and with no rhyme and reason, and possibly finding everyone unprepared and defenceless. This is an apocalyptic fear where we feel that our whole existence is threatened.[12]

This short history of fear has taught us that the fate of humans involves being susceptible to danger, which leaves us with a feeling of insecurity. The problem is that the world is full of dangers that may strike at any time and with little or no warning. Probability, even if we calculate it to the best of our abilities, offers no certainty that the most awful dangers or threats could be or could not be avoided in *this* case here and now or *that* case there and then, as Nassim Nicholas Taleb has pointed out, in *The Black Swan* and *Antifragile*.[13] All in all, the human condition implies that we know of death's inescapability and therefore face the awesome task of trying to survive the acquisition of that knowledge. For human beings, fear is a faithful companion as we try to navigate the task of living with the awareness of death's inevitability. We live on a planet characterized by human interdependence, and this simply makes fear part of the rule book.

THE CASE AGAINST FEAR

American philosopher Martha Nussbaum has argued that the appeal to fear is problematic because it easily gives rise to scapegoating, or other ways of demonizing the other. Her case against fear goes beyond the simple claim of FDR that the only fear we should fear is fear itself. According to Nussbaum, Roosevelt was wrong, at least if we were to take his words literally. There are indeed things beyond fear that we need to fear, like the rise of Nazism. Nussbaum's case against fear is a case against a certain kind of fear. Nussbaum's account of the negative effects of fear departs from the figure of the absolute monarch. To her, the political appeal to fear is closely connected to despotism and one-man rule.

Fear requires careful scrutiny and containment, Nussbaum has suggested. Her argument against the appeal to fear is directed against the sort of appeal which is hasty and leads to panic. This sort of appeal to fear often demands ultimate loyalty, like in a war situation. The problem with that kind of fear is that it has a way of running ahead of careful thought, Nussbaum warns.

The baseline of Nussbaum's critique is that the appeal to fear may threaten rationality. Or better, it establishes alternative rationality, with not enough time to consider the reality of options. The purpose of Nussbaum's argument is to safeguard the virtue of keeping sane in times of stress, what we so far have called a "crisis." Fear is the opposite of trust, she claims, and in a liberal democracy trust is needed to connect citizens. The horizontal trust in a liberal democracy stands in contrast to the vertical fear of a monarch's punishment. This fear in turn ensures the ruler's compliance, as he requires absolute obedience from the subjects. Instead of mutual trust between citizens, the monarch is left with fearful people who want protection and care.[14] Nussbaum's arguments are convincing to some extent, but her treatment of fear rests on a narrow notion of fear. Even a democratic leader may have to appeal to fear in the face of crisis. The same accounts for a business leader striving to argue which path to pursue when the future of the company appears perilous.

However, Nussbaum's reflection on the problematic aspects of fear reminds us that appealing to fear appears morally questionable to many. Others would go even further and claim that any appeal to fear fosters hatred and mistrust. They would point to leaders in politics and business who appear deliberately divisive in their rhetoric to promote their own cause and who use disinformation to create irrational, and ill-founded appeals to fear. Although the feeling of fear is a fundamental human experience, one still needs to ask if the appeal to fear could end up being rhetorically ineffective, perhaps even "bad" in a moral sense.

In an authoritarian, political climate, there is obviously more room for this sort of demagogue rhetoric. Appealing to collective fear, such as the likelihood of terrorist attacks, aggression from an unfriendly neighbour state, or the next pandemic, could strengthen an authoritarian mindset. Would an appeal to this sort of mentality include a call for a strong leader, and emphasis on strict rules and regulations, harsher punishments for those who break the rules, isolationism, and intolerance? The effect of such appeals to collective fear can therefore easily be exploited by political entrepreneurs and tyrants who may want to use a crisis to install more authoritarian measures.

In political communication, "fearmongering" or "scaremongering" are terms describing a manipulative way of communicating. This sort of appeal wants to cause fear by using exaggerated rumours of impending danger. For those who use the term, the problem with fearmongering is its fundamentally irrational basis. It appeals to fear the wrong things at the wrong time. The attention and resources are used to avoid rather rare and unlikely dangers. The result is that more probable dangers could be ignored. An example from the domestic area of life may help us understand the irrational basis of fearmongering. We know that some parents would teach their children to watch out for white vans to avoid being abducted, failing to teach their children to pay attention to more common dangers such as unhealthy food, a destructive lifestyle, or regular traffic accidents.

The case against fear has yet another argument to consider: If the speaker is taken to appeal to fear, the speaker may be dismissed as having an illegitimate argument. Why is this so? Because appealing to fear is found to be somewhat suspicious by many with democratic instincts, it is possible to dismiss the legitimacy of a particular political project by linking it to fear. If a speaker claims that her opponent appeals to fear in an unnecessary or ill-founded manner, she may discharge the validity of a particular argument. Several polarized debates lately are examples of this dynamic, like the Scottish independence referendum (2013), Britain's EU membership referendum (2016), and debates on the COVID-19-pandemic restriction and discussions on climate change. If you label a political purpose or political adversary "project fear," you have also made it easier for the public to disregard the arguments presented.[15]

As important as these claims are, in this book, however, our aim is to consider how a *well-founded* appeal to fear may be constructive. Such an appeal to fear needs to be adequate and rational in a certain sense.

The appeal has to offer an account of reality and present it in a persuasive manner. Identifying the key elements of a crisis is a rhetorical challenge. It is usually something very practical: How should a leader facing company bankruptcy speak to address fear? What sort of rhetorical repertoire is fitting for a leader of a state facing a national emergency? How should a climate change activist present new research evidence to the public?

Every crisis forces the leader and her followers to ask whether some fears are more important than others. If the answer is yes, which it usually is, the leader needs to provide a persuasive account of reality and argue why a certain course of action appears justified. In a crisis, a leader may have to consider whether the fear of fascism is more important or less important than the fear of environmental extinction. Or put more provocatively, could the fear of environmental extinction imply that we might need to deploy partially anti-democratic measures to combat the problem?

The dichotomy between fear and trust that Nussbaum sets up is also worth questioning. To install trust as the guideline for human communication seems reassuring, but in the face of a crisis, one needs to take account of the situation at hand. This may imply an appeal to fear. Such an appeal may even be essential in gaining the trust of a particular audience. Perhaps trust and fear are not by necessity opposites? We will argue that appealing to fear does not necessarily run contrary to loving the good, hoping for the future, and combating evil.

Implicit in Nussbaum's critique of the appeal to fear is the assumption that an emphasis on fear may be an obstacle for an open and democratic conversation. By demonizing your adversary, you may hinder a fruitful, public exchange of opinion. Nussbaum´s argument that a certain way to appeal to fear may paralyze the rational exchange of arguments, carries some weight, indeed, as we have argued above when we discussed fear-mongering and the dangers of demagogue rhetoric in the face of a crisis. However, against Nussbaum one could object that her account of reality appears too optimistic. Put bluntly, if there is evil in the world, both in an apocalyptic, political, and private sense, then it may be adequate to appeal to fear.

Politically, what comes to mind is the rationale of a defence alliance like NATO. The idea of NATO is built on deterrence and retaliation, clearly explicated in article 5 of the NATO charter, which states that an armed attack against one or more of the member states shall be considered an attack against all members and consequently result in a collective response, which may include the use of armed force.[16] Deterrence is a military strategy where the intention is to frighten an adversary from aggression. The key instrument of the strategy is the threat of reprisal, which may prevent an aggressive neighbour state from doing something that another state might desire. Either way, fear is not just a thing for cowards. The proof of the pudding when appealing to fear is always: does the speaker summon her audience to fear the right things at the right time?

EVERY SITUATION IS POTENT WITH FEAR

Fear is often found to be an existential emotion. However, our interest in fear is not mainly an interest in fear as a psychological phenomenon, but we are concerned with how words may create fear. The appeal to fear often aims to persuade the listener of a certain course of action. The speaker may employ an appeal to fear to argue for a preferred future vision or instigate the importance of certain thoughts or actions. A newly elected head of state could appeal to stand together against the forces that want to "tear our democracy apart." The visionary leader of a climate activist NGO could frame the current climate crisis as "a moment of truth, where we need to decide what kind of story we want to tell our grandchildren." Both the head of state and the NGO leader appeal to feelings. Appealing to feelings is essential to the art of persuasion. If you want to forward a certain purpose, ideal, or cause, you must appeal to emotions that may change or move the minds and actions of your audience. However, this does not imply that the appeal is irrational.

When we consider the appeal to fear, we need to take note of two different ways to address the role of emotions in the life of humans. For Aristotle and people following the Greek philosopher, emotions like fear are essential. They are almost like set categories. Such emotions are, as we have already argued, an inevitable part of the human condition. As feelings, they are of course open to interpretation, but they cannot be ignored. However, for the Roman Philosopher Seneca, and psychological constructivists following the Stoic tradition and Freud, emotions may be processed rationally. Their impact may potentially be ignored or controlled. The Stoic approach presupposes a more elastic take on emotions like fear. Their point is that a feeling is a sort of construct, which may be eliminated or reduced by rational thinking. In other words, the human person can choose not to be ridden by fear.

From a rhetorical perspective, fear is something elastic and flexible. Our aim in this book is to explore the metaphorical bandwidth of appealing to fear during crisis. Our selective focus is on a particular crisis, the ongoing energy crisis, but the study aims to offer relevant and analytical insights for any appeal to fear in a crisis. We ask what options a speaker has when faced with a crisis and explore how an appeal to fear may serve a constructive purpose.

Hierarchies of Fear

The appeal to fear comes with the call to make a choice: Which fears are most important, and how should one react based on the appeal to fear? Some scholars of psychology propose a hierarchy of fears, a set of basic fears out of which all other fears are manufactured. Psychologist Karl Albrecht has described five basic fears in a "feararchy"—extinction, mutilation, loss of autonomy, separation, and ego-death.[17] The typology we present in this book bears some similarities to other hierarchies of fear, but it still offers something distinct. The distinction between the three different appeals to fear—apocalyptic, political, and private—reflects the situational and temporal appeal to different kinds of fear in a given situation: We focus on how the crisis at hand calls for an appeal to apocalyptic, political, or private fear, or perhaps all three of them, but in different ways and on different levels. The point is that the typology of the three fears equips a leader with a rhetorical bandwidth to use in a crisis.

Fear is not just a state of mind. It is a phenomenon with some sort of reference to the real world. Fear has an intentional object. However, human fear is not necessarily corresponding to matters in a proportional manner. Our perception of a particular threat may be influenced by the appeal to fear. Similarly, our hierarchy of fears is altered when life around us changes.

However, for an appeal to a particular fear to be effective or even "successful," in the sense that it achieves prominence, the speaker has to take the perceived reality and cultural setting into account. Where Seneca might point out that the fear of losing your child is irrational, as your children are destined to die at some point anyhow, most cultures find that it is right to fear the loss of a child. Numerous Hollywood movies tell the stories of heroes and heroines who have fought to save their children from danger. The bottom line, fear may be used for rhetorical purposes.

When we consider a hierarchy of fears, it is worth comparing the hierarchies of fear to Abrahams Maslow's much used, but also thoroughly critiqued, concept of the hierarchy of needs. In 1943 Abraham Maslow proposed a hierarchy of needs to explain how humans partake in behavioural motivation. Maslow distinguished between basic needs, psychological needs, and self-fulfilment needs. The basic needs, at the bottom of Maslow's hierarchy, are physiological needs like food, water, warmth, and rest, and safety needs like the feeling of security. The psychological needs are the needs for intimate relationship and friendship and the demand for recognition, esteem, and accomplishment. The self-fulfilment needs are the creative activity of humans where we strive to achieve our full potential. The classification system, Maslow argued, reflects the universal need of establishing a societal foundation first, based on the basic needs, and then proceeding to more acquired emotions.[18] The problem with Maslow's pyramid is found in its deterministic and static framing. A rhetorical framing of needs or fears presupposes a more elastic perception of reality. What counts as the most important need or fear depends on time and place.

The three fears that we explore in this book are situated fears. In our typology, we distinguish between fears concerning nature, political life, and the self. The first appeal to fear is the appeal to an *apocalyptic* fear (T0). This is when we fear that our world may be annihilated and that human beings may be facing extinction. Both in the case of a potential nuclear threat and the imminent emergence of a catastrophic climate crisis, such an appeal may appear justified. Secondly, you have the appeal to political fear. It is the fear that our civilization and our society, as we know it, may be coming to an end, or is being replaced by another order. Thirdly, you have the appeal to private fear. This is the fear that your house is on fire, in the sense that your sense of self is threatened, perhaps because you fear losing your job or fear a breach in your moral self, your feeling of being true to yourself.

A Rhetoric of Fear?

In this book, we draw on classical, rhetorical theory to reflect on the appeal to fear during a crisis. We explore what happens when a speaker appeals to a particular audience, at a particular time, and at a particular place. It could be a CEO, who fears that the company is less than fit to meet the challenges of the emerging green economy. It could be a leader of a climate activist NGO, driven by the fear that the public is unable to fully comprehend the consequences of the ongoing climate crisis, and that she is unable to persuade them to change their behaviour to save the planet. It could be a political leader, realizing the need to shift to a greener economy, but who is still sort of paralysed by the threat that the economy may stagnate, and that the country will face rising unemployment and public protest. It could even be the manager of a well-known sports team, with a brand heavily relying on financial support from a sponsor, which builds their success on fossil resources.

All these leaders must relate to fear in different fashions, and they must think of ways to appear credible and convincing when they communicate with their audiences and relate to the imminent presence of fear. But what should rhetoric of fear look like, apart from something many leaders think they should avoid? As rhetoric deals with the art of persuasion, we need to take the world of the listeners into account, if we want to know more about how a leader should speak well in a given context.

However, the world of the listeners is not a world in mere harmony. Every situation is potent with fear. As a leader, you have to deal with conflict and crisis, and you have to face your own fear and the fear of others. In this book, we will be looking at actual speeches by a wide range of leaders, from the world of politics, business, NGOs, sports, and other spheres of society. With the help of the analytical tools of the classical, rhetorical tradition, we will identify the main elements of persuasion when a speaker appeals to fear.

When we use rhetorical theory to analyse speeches, we need to be attentive to what the speaker showcases, but we also need to be alert to what the speaker leaves out, to persuade the audience of a certain argument or meaning. The crucial point here is that only the leader who is perceived as credible and authentic can persuade an audience with authority. When a leader is perceived as credible, he speaks the truth. From a rhetorical perspective, the truth is both historical and situational. The rhetorical take on truth therefore differs from the philosophical take on truth. As a speaker you must, and you should, adapt to your follow-ers' situation, but only to a certain point, if you still want to appear trustworthy and truthful. To persuade the audience the speaking leader therefore has three means of persuasion he may use—*ethos, logos, pathos*. These are three basic elements of any communication theory, namely that there is a *speaker*, a *message*, and a *listener*. First, the speaker needs to reflect on how his or her character, his *ethos*, appears to the audience.

Secondly, the leader has to use the message, the *logos*, as a means of persuasion. Finally, the speaking leader has to appeal to the feelings of the audience, the *pathos*, to speak persuasively. These rhetorical and moral considerations are of uttermost importance, even when we try to develop a rhetoric of fear fitting for a leader who wants to speak with authority and appear credible during crisis.

When you speak to influence and persuade, you speak with the aim to move your listeners in a particular direction. It is therefore essential to relate to where people are at. Even an appeal to change or to shift direction benefits from a convincing interpretation of the audience's perception of reality. The leader needs to name reality in a persuasive manner. If the audience is struck by apocalyptic fear, you need to somehow address that fear. If your listeners are worried about their jobs, you need to speak to that uneasiness in a convincing way. All leadership is directed to the future and therefore involves change, but it starts by addressing the *place* of the audience, and their current perception of reality. How we perceive fear is closely linked to our perception of change. The ancient Greeks regarded the earthly condition as a place marked by change, suffering, and ultimately death. A key concept in their understanding of human destiny was *pathos* or passion. Feelings, and passions, were as transitory as human beings, and they were contrasted with the ideal world, the *apathic* nature of the gods. All good speeches, therefore, had to address this breach that human beings experience.

THE APPEAL TO FEAR AS A MORAL AND RHETORICAL DILEMMA

As we develop a rhetoric of fear, we are faced with a moral dilemma: You have probably heard the phrase "this is mere rhetoric." The saying stems from an ancient, ethical conflict. The Sophists found that rhetoric was like money, a mere instrument for the speaker to achieve his own defined goal. From this perspective, rhetoric is a technical tool only concerned with efficiency. Plato and Aristotle on the other hand argued that this approach is highly problematic. Their point was that rhetoric, like all other arts, has to do with morality. When you speak, your speech should serve a higher goal: truth, goodness, beauty, and above all, justice.

That a well-founded speech should connect to a higher end is a crucial, moral consideration to take into account as we try to develop a rhetoric that helps the speaker to appeal to fear in an adequate manner. Even when a company is hit by a major crisis, the CEO may appeal to a set of higher virtues that the company's purpose is associated with. If you represent a traditional business, you may promote patience and perseverance as company virtues that will bring you through the storm. If your company is a green economy start-up, the leader of the company may appeal to the beauty of the company's future vision, or perhaps even better, the just cause that the company is dedicated to fight for.

Calibrating the appeal to fear requires sound judgement and an evaluation of the current reality. It depends on what you see, and how you tell the story of the things you see. Let us consider again the rhetorical and moral dilemma of the pre-WWII situation in Britain. Sir Winston Churchill and Neville Chamberlain are often portrayed as counterparts. The conflict between the two peaked on the verge of the outbreak of the Second World War, in 1938 and 1939. It reminds us of the importance of assessing the situation.

Unlike Chamberlain, Churchill had a very clear hierarchy of fears. He feared Nazism above anything, as he saw it as a path to human extinction, not just the destruction of Great Britain, but of humanity as such. In hindsight we realize that Churchill's advantage versus Chamberlain was that he defined his leadership by dealing with one particular fear. To Churchill, the fear of being bombed away from independence, and ultimately the fear of human extinction if the Nazi ideology were to rule the world, took prominence over all other fears in his rhetorical approach to the situation.

For Neville Chamberlain, the situation was more complex. Chamberlain loathed war. He wanted to believe that it was possible to make a peace treaty with Hitler, and he tried to convince the people of Britain that he was right. Chamberlain prioritized the fear of war over the fear that Churchill may be right in not trusting Hitler's promises.

It is hard to put oneself in the shoes of either Churchill or Chamberlain. It is not easy to determine which speech you would have given if you were faced with a similar challenge. What may seem like an obvious choice of rhetoric when we assess history from a privileged position, was perhaps less obvious in 1938. Churchill's fear of Nazism does not come by itself. It required the fine development of discernment and judgement, a rhetorical consideration of the situation at hand.

Fundamentally, rhetoric aims to teach the speaker the art of speaking well. The art of persuasion, therefore, starts with the presupposition that the one who speaks well, thinks well. Speaking well involves more than simply speaking correctly. It is also more than just presenting a subject matter or a "truth." Speaking well means speaking aptly, *aptum* in Latin. It concerns the speaker's ability to craft a message that appears fitting with the time, place, and audience at hand. This is a capacity that needs continuous reflection and practice.

FEAR IS

The first story of this book is the story about fear. We argue that appealing to fear is inevitable when something's at stake. When you are in the midst of a crisis, portraying fear as an illusion may be correct, but it is not always adequate. Reality has a sneaky tendency to push back. Our basic assumption in the book is therefore that fear is at play when and where something is at stake.

For a speech to be effective, the speaker must make a convincing account of reality, and appeal to fear in an adequate way, based on that account. A mayor of a city susceptible to floods, perhaps caused by climate change, needs to take the townspeople's feelings of fear into account. The CEO of an oil company facing the threat of stiff competition must somehow address that fear.

The appeal to fear is always a situational plea. Simply put, an appeal to fear is justified if the situation calls for it. The appeal to fear is the speaker who proclaims that right now and right here it is relevant to fear a particular thing, more than other potential fears. Naming reality in this manner presents the audience with a rationally founded and rhetorical choice. The appeal to fear requires a response. The presented dilemma, the dilemma of fear, requires an answer.

NOTES

1. FDR inauguration speech March 4, 1933: https://avalon.law.yale.edu/20th_century/froos1.asp.
2. Neville Chamberlain "Peace for our time"-speech: https://eudocs.lib.byu.edu/index.php/Neville_Chamberlain%27s_%22Peace_For_Our_Time%22_speech, http://www.emersonkent.com/speeches/peace_in_our_time.htm and http://news.bbc.co.uk/onthisday/hi/dates/stories/september/30/newsid_3115000/3115476.stm.
3. Aristotle: *Rhetoric*. Mineola, New York: Dover, 2004.
4. Rousseau, Jean-Jacques: *The Social Contract*. New York: Peter Eckler Publisher, 1893.

5. Aristotle: *Poetics*, available at: http://www.perseus.tufts.edu/hopper/text? doc=Perseus:abo:tlg,0086,034:1453b.

6. Augustine: *Confessions* (Transl. by Henry Chadwick). Oxford: Oxford University Press, 1992. Augustine: De Civitate Dei, *The City of God*, books I–XIII available at: https://www.gutenberg.org/files/45304/ 45304-h/45304-h.htm.

7. Machiavelli, Niccolò: *The Prince*. Charleston: Biblolife, 2008.

8. Hankiss, Elemér: *Fears and Symbols*. Budapest: Central European University Press, 2001, 6–7.

9. Bauman, Zygmunt: *Liquid Fear*. Cambridge: Polity Press, 2007, 4–7.

10. Darwin, Charles: *The Origin of Species by Means of Natural Selection*. London: Penguin books, 1985. First published by John Murray in 1859, 129.

11. On the Titanic Syndrome in business: https://www.mindspace.me/mag azine/2019-11-30_the-titanic-syndrome%E2%80%8A-%E2%80%8Amind space.

12. Bauman, Zygmunt: *Liquid Fear*. Cambridge: Polity Press, 2007, 3–4, 17.

13. Taleb, Nassim Nicholas: *Antifragile: Things that Gain from Disorder*. New York: Random House, 2014, and Taleb, Nassim Nicholas: *The Black Swan*. New York: Random House, 2010.

14. Nussbaum, Martha: *The Monarchy of Fear: A Philosopher Looks at Our Political Crisis*. New York: Simon & Schuster Paperbacks, 2018.

15. On the roots of "project fear," see for instance: https://www.theguardian. com/commentisfree/2016/mar/11/project-fear-started-as-a-silly-pri vate-joke-now-it-wont-go-away, https://www.independent.co.uk/news/ uk/politics/the-campaign-to-stay-in-the-eu-is-project-fear-says-boris-joh nson-a6903216.html, and https://www.telegraph.co.uk/politics/2020/ 09/28/project-fear-tory-mp-silenced-commons-furious-rebuke-whitty/, and https://www.lse.ac.uk/granthaminstitute/news/mp-joins-climate- change-deniers-project-fear-on-net-zero/.

16. The NATO treaty: https://www.nato.int/cps/en/natohq/official_texts_ 17120.htm.

17. An account of Karl Albrecht's typology of five basic fears: https://www. psychologytoday.com/intl/blog/brainsnacks/201203/the-only-5-fears- we-all-share.

18. Maslow, Abraham: "A theory of human motivation." In *Psychological Review*, 50(4), 370–396, 1943.

BIBLIOGRAPHY

Aristotle: *Poetics*, available at: http://www.perseus.tufts.edu/hopper/text?doc=
Perseus:abo:tlg,0086,034:1453b.

Aristotle: *Rhetoric*. Mineola, New York: Dover, 2004.

Arendt, Hannah: *The Human Condition*. Chicago: The University of Chicago
Press, 1998.

Beck, Ulrich: *World at Risk*. Cambridge: Polity Press, 2007.

Bauman, Zygmunt: *Liquid Fear*. Cambridge: Polity Press, 2007.

Cialdini, Robert: *Influence, New and Expanded: The Psychology of Persuasion*. New
York: Harper Business, 2021.

Darwin, Charles: *The Origin of Species by Means of Natural Selection*. London:
Penguin books, 1985. First published by John Murray in 1859.

Enos, Richard Leo & Thompson, Roger, et al. (eds.): *The Rhetoric of St. Augustine of Hippo. De Doctrina Christiana & the Search for a Distinctly Christian
Rhetoric*. Waco: Baylor University Press, 2008.

Farnsworth, Ward: *Farnsworth's Classical English Rhetoric*. Jaffrey: David R.
Godine, 2011.

Fafner, Jørgen: *Tanke og tale. Den retoriske tradition i Vesteuropa*. Copenhagen:
C. A. Reitzel, 1978.

Hankiss, Elemér: *Fears and Symbols*. Budapest: Central European University
Press, 2001.

Humes, James C: *The Sir Winston Method. Five Secrets of Speaking the Language
of Leadership*. New York: William Morrow & Company, 1991.

Kennedy, George: *The Art of Rhetoric in the Roman World 300 B.C.—A.D. 300*.
Eugene, OR: Wipf and Stock, 2008.

Kennedy, George: *Classical Rhetoric and its Christian and Secular Tradition from
Ancient to Modern Times*. Chapel Hill: University of North Carolina Press,
1999.

Kjeldsen, Jens E.: *Hva er retorikk?* Oslo: Universitetsforlaget, 2014.

Lausberg, Heinrich, et al. (ed.): *Handbook of Literary Rhetoric: A Foundation of
Literary Study*. Leiden: Brill, 2002.

Machiavelli, Niccolò: *The Prince*. Charleston: Biblolife, 2008.

Mack, Peter: *A History of Renaissance Rhetoric 1380–1620*. Oxford: Oxford
University Press, 2011.

Müller, Gerhard; Balz, Horst and Krause, Gerhard (eds.): *Theologische Realenzyklopädie* (36 volumes). De Gruyter, Berlin, 1976–2004.

Norheim, Bård & Haga, Joar: *The Four Speeches. Every Leader Has to Know*.
London: Palgrave Macmillan (Palgrave Pivot), 2020.

Nussbaum, Martha: *The Monarchy of Fear: A Philosopher Looks at Our Political
Crisis*. New York: Simon & Schuster Paperbacks, 2018.

Quintillian: *The Orator's Education. Volume V: Books 11–12* (Ed. And Transl. by Donald A. Russell). Harvard: Harvard University Press, Loeb Classical Library.

Pernot, Laurent: *Epideictic Rhetoric. Questioning the Stakes of Ancient Praise.* Austin: University of Texas Press, 2015.

Svendsen, Lars Fr H.: *Frykt.* Oslo: Universitetsforlaget, 2007.

Taleb, Nassim Nicholas: *Antifragile: Things that Gain from Disorder.* New York: Random House, 2014.

Taleb, Nassim Nicholas: *The Black Swan.* New York: Random House, 2010.

Ueding, Gert (ed.): *Historisches Wörterbuch der Rhetorik.* (12 volumes). Berlin/New York: Walter de Gruyter, 2015.

Vestrheim, Gjert: *Klassisk retorikk.* Oslo: Dreyers forlag, 2018.

Vickers, Brian: *In Defense of Rhetoric.* Cambridge: Clarendon Press, 1988.

Yukl, Gary: *Leadership in Organizations* (8th edition). New Jersey: Pearson, 2013.

Two Stories: One Dilemma

Abstract The second chapter presents the reader with two different stories. First, we tell the story of the three kinds of fear, and how they relate to three different places—nature, culture, and the place we call home. Secondly, we contrast the story of the three fears with the history of the ongoing energy crisis and how it has shaped and still shapes our feeling of fear in multiple ways. The second chapter analyses speeches by Jimmy Carter, George Bush Sr, Greta Thunberg, and Barack Obama. Reflecting on the history of the emerging energy and climate crisis and how it relates to the story of fear, the chapter ends by exploring how our perceptions of the world as a limited or limitless place shape our concept of fear.

Keywords Apocalyptic fear · Political fear · Private fear · Energy crisis · Climate change · Climate crisis · Global warming · The American dream · Bretton Woods · Oil

THE FIRST STORY: A STORY OF THREE KINDS OF FEAR

Human beings fear a lot of different things. We may fear that we lack enough energy and food supply to make it through tomorrow. Or we may fear that criminals will rob our house while we are away on holiday. We

B. Norheim and J. Haga, *The Three Fears Every Leader Has to Know*, https://doi.org/10.1007/978-3-031-08984-8_2

may even fear that our grandchildren will inherit a world that is impossible to inhabit. In the first chapter of the book, we argued that humans operate with elastic hierarchies of fears. Some fears are simply more prominent than others, depending on the situation. A crisis, like the corona pandemic or a migration crisis, may alter our hierarchies of fear. The most urgent dilemma for a speaking leader during a crisis is the following: When there are multiple fears at play, which fear should be prioritized in the appeal to your listeners?

The typology of fear that this book presents describes three ideal types of fear that exist on a continuum:

T0:   *Apocalyptic* fear
T1:   *Political* fear
T2:   *Private* fear

In other words, the three fears may exist alongside each other in a crisis. A leader needs to consider and prioritize which fear to appeal to. Throughout the book, the reader is challenged to identify how situational features of the three ideal fears are at play.

The purpose of the typology is to help the speaking leader to reflect on how to use fear constructively. As we have seen, this implies assessing the fears at play in a particular situation. The typology also invites the reader to reflect on how the speaker should be positioned when addressing fear. What is the fitting character to take on as you appeal to a particular fear? Our aim is to offer a framework for leaders to reflect on the appeal to fear when a minor or major crisis strikes. However, it is important to note that this typology of the three fears does not offer a moral chart for action.

THE SECOND STORY: OIL, WE NEED OIL!

On July 15, 1979, the American President, Jimmy Carter spoke live on national television. The speech later became known as "the crisis of confidence"-speech. Carter told the story of the ongoing energy crisis, declaring to the American public that "we believed that our nation's resources were limitless until 1973, when we had to face a growing dependence on foreign oil."[1] The fear Carter described is the fear of being dependent upon the energy supply of foreign, and sometimes hostile, states.

The industrial world's dependence on oil has long made a huge impact on national and international politics. Whereas coal was the major energy source driving the industrial revolution in its beginning years after the invention of the Watt steam engine, oil supplanted coal from the late nineteenth century, particularly in the United States. When mass-produced cars, like the first T-Ford in 1908, were made economically accessible to the public in general, refined motor fuel oil became the predominant use of oil. During World War I, the use of oil proved to be a key component in modern warfare, fuelling ships, land vehicles, and planes.

The request for oil increased because of the war, and new markets emerged. As a result of this, American oil companies started to show interest in oil concessions in the Middle East in the early 1920s, when the fear of oil shortage was widespread. However, towards the end of the 1920s, the fear of oil shortage had been replaced by a surplus of oil. International oil companies then turned their attention to limiting outputs and administering the global oil markets, instead of competing for the development of oil resources. Technological advancements and increasing oil production in many parts of the world led to another round of overproduction of oil at the beginning of the 1930s. Throughout the remains of the 1930s governments began to pursue a more active role in the oil industry, auguring a wave of oil nationalizations in the decades following World War II.

At the beginning of the war, the United States was responsible for 60% of the world's oil production, followed by Russia and Venezuela. Japan was heavily dependent on US oil, and Japan's attack on the Pacific fleet at Pearl Harbor in December 1941 was at least partially motivated by the access to oil and the fear of running out of oil. The US had cut oil supplies to Japan during the Northern hemisphere summer of 1941, following Japan's invasion of Indochina. The post-WWII era manifested the United States as an oil-fuelled, global superpower, supplying oil and energy aid to a devastated Europe.

In the post-WWII era access to oil and free transportation of oil to emerging markets has played a key role in many international conflicts, like the Suez crisis in 1956. The conflict started when Egypt nationalized the Suez Canal. At that time half of the canal's traffic was petroleum-based. During the 1960s the Arab nations were increasingly offended by a market largely determined by Western oil companies and their oil price cuts and US import caps. This also kept prices low. In September 1960 representatives from Saudi Arabia, Venezuela, Kuwait, Qatar, and Iran met in Baghdad with Iraqi officials, representing 80% of the world's crude exports. The Organization of the Petroleum Exporting Nations (OPEC) was formed on September 14, 1960, with the purpose to defend oil prices.

The Six-Day War was an armed conflict with Israel on one side and Egypt, Syria, and Jordan on the other side. On June 17, 1967, the second day of the war, Arab oil ministers called for an oil embargo on any country friendly to Israel. Although oil shipments to the United States and Great Britain was halted, the increase in US domestic oil production largely compensated for the loss. The announced embargo was lifted in September of the same year, and the fear of running out of oil was no longer as imminent.

The embargo in 1967 was a sort of prelude to the worldwide oil crisis in 1973. In April 1973 President Richard Nixon announced that he would end the US limits on oil import. At the outbreak of the Yom Kippur War in October 1973, the United States was therefore much more vulnerable to reduced oil supplies. Syria and Egypt attacked Israel on the Jewish holy Day Yom Kippur on October 6, 1973. On October 19, the Nixon administration announced a huge military aid package to Israel, upon which Arab states responded by suspending oil shipments to nations supportive of Israel. Within a few months, gasoline prices in the United States increased by 40%. In not too long, consumers in Europe, Japan, and the US started to panic over the oil shortage. Gas rationing and long lines at gas stations became commonplace.

The second Arab oil embargo came to an end in March 1974. The problem with the price control measures that were taken by national governments, was that they also halted the profitability of domestic oil production.

During the 1970s the fear of running out of oil became a fear that determined many political measures taken. An oil-fuelled economy was not just essential to ensure continued economic growth, but the oil-fuelled economy also proved its vulnerability. Fear and vulnerability are often closely connected. A feeling of vulnerability may be linked to the feeling of being dependent on others. After the Iranian revolution at the beginning of 1979, panic once again struck over oil-supply shortage as oil prices soon doubled and hour-long lines in front of gas stations returned. It is against the backdrop of these political events that President Jimmy Carter addressed the American nation on national television and delivered his "crisis of confidence"-speech in July 1979. Here Carter announced more energy conservation measures and a phase out of oil price controls.

He also promised a political road map with the aim to become independent of foreign oil suppliers. At the same time, he admonished the nation for worshipping "self-indulgence and consumption."[2]

The years that have followed since 1973 have brought a variety of political crises, where the supply of oil and fluctuating oil prices have been key factor. If we fast forward to the beginning of the 1990s, we see how oil once again became a determining factor in an armed conflict. In a speech on August 8, 1990, President George H. W. Bush described Iraq's aggression as an economic threat to the United States and the rest of the world:

> The stakes are high. Iraq is already a rich and powerful country that possesses the world's second largest reserves of oil and over a million men under arms. It's the fourth largest military in the world. Our country now imports nearly half the oil it consumes and could face a major threat to its economic independence. Much of the world is even more dependent upon imported oil and is even more vulnerable to Iraqi threats.[3]

In describing the magnitude of the threat, President Bush did not hold back and compared the rule of Saddam Hussein to the rule of dictators in the 1930s:

> But if history teaches us anything, it is that we must resist aggression, or it will destroy our freedoms. Appeasement does not work. As was the case in the 1930's, we see in Saddam Hussein an aggressive dictator threatening his neighbors. Only 14 days ago, Saddam Hussein promised his friends he would not invade Kuwait. And 4 days ago, he promised the world he would withdraw. And twice we have seen what his promises mean: His promises mean nothing.

Bush appealed to a political fear, where the continued rule of Hussein represented a threat to human civilization. Taking his lesson from history, Bush wanted to appear not as a Chamberlain seeking appeasement, but as a Churchill refusing to believe the dictator's promises. Therefore, Bush used the speech to make an appeal to other oil-producing nations "to do what they can to increase production in order to minimize any impact that oil flow reductions will have on the world economy." Even the oil companies were exhorted to do "their fair share," and "not abuse today's uncertainties to raise prices." The President also reminded his listeners of the suffering and costs that may follow from challenging Iraq's invasion of Kuwait, highlighting "bravery" as the fitting response to the fear that Saddam Hussein's rule installed:

> Standing up for our principles will not come easy. It may take time and possibly cost a great deal. But we are asking no more of anyone than of the brave young men and women of our Armed Forces and their families. And I ask that in the churches around the country prayers be said for those who are committed to protect and defend America's interests.

Towards the end of the speech Bush employed a grand style of speech to persuade of the imminent political fear caused by the invasion of Kuwait: Bush tried to make a convincing argument for warfare against Iraq. Bush here explored the loftier registers of political oratory, personalizing America as "she," which also makes any sacrifice for America personal, and potentially more worthy and noble:

> Standing up for our principle is an American tradition. As it has so many times before, it may take time and tremendous effort, but most of all, it will take unity of purpose. As I've witnessed throughout my life in both war and peace, America has never wavered when her purpose is driven by principle. And in this August day, at home and abroad, I know she will do no less.

Bush's emphasis on "principle" may be seen as an appeal to America's legacy of freedom. Appealing to a strong "legacy" is usually a very effective way of naming a greater "we," a community worthy of dedication and sacrifice.

In the last decades, the industrial world's dependence on oil has faced a change in public opinion. Oil is not simply the black gold fuelling an economy of growth and offering unlimited promises for the future. The use of oil has increasingly become a suspect source of energy. Starting with the Exxon Valdez oil spill in 1989 and later with the climate protocol of the Kyoto Meeting in 1997, the world's dependence on oil has become the carrier of an apocalyptic fear. Some fear that our dependence on oil will ultimately lead to our self-destruction.[4]

GO WEST!

Sweet dreams were once made of oil. We have seen how the supply of oil played a particularly essential role in fuelling the progress of the American dream. The American dream is the belief that anyone, regardless of their background, can be successful. It portrays a society of limitless opportunities for those who are willing to work hard and make the necessary sacrifices to move upwards. The American dream relates to a Western political vision of democracy: the belief that the world is endless or limitless. It is the call to go west to find and conquer new land.

We used to think that our world was limitless. America is the ultimate representation of that grand narrative, as it brands itself as the land of endless opportunities. America extends an invitation to all the world's entrepreneurs and mercenaries. "Go west, and you will find gold and fertile soil!" The American dream is built on the idea of expansion and mastering and dominion of the new world, and even the universe. Man on the moon is therefore just an upgraded version of the go west-story. Finding oil, lots of oil, becomes a confirmation of the "go west"-narrative at work.

With the climate crisis, the "go west"-narrative is fundamentally challenged. The climate crisis makes us acquainted with the fear that the world's resources are limited. The world may not be a world of endless opportunities. Nature may strike back unless we learn from our failures and show moderation. The energy crisis represents an immense shift of narrative. This also influences how we interpret fear: Our dependence on oil makes us realize that the world is limited. The fossil resource itself reminds us that we inhabit a limited world. From an American perspective, however, the story of the limited resource, oil or energy, has changed since the 1970s. Why was it possible for Trump to negotiate peace in the Middle East? Well, simply put, follow the money: Since Carter's talk in 1979 the tables have been turned. Approaching 2020, the United States had become self-supplied with oil and was able to control its lines of supply.

HOW DARE YOU GO WEST!

However, a new problem emerges if you simply focus on energy supply. What is more frightening; the fear of being reliant on the energy supply from a foreign power or the fear of global warming? As the climate crisis has taken over for the A-bomb as the one problem that may bring about human extinction, political leaders are forced to navigate this dilemma. Appealing to the fear of future global warming is a challenging rhetorical enterprise: Just as love is all around, and fear is all around, even climate is all around. Where the A-bomb is something very concrete, the climate crisis is both imminent and distant, and therefore the climate crisis is harder to fear.

So how do you appeal to fear in a constructive and well-founded way when you speak about the climate crisis? On September 23, 2019, young Swedish climate change activist Greta Thunberg spoke at the UN Climate Action Summit in New York. Thunberg's intense, prophetic appeal caught global attention:

> You have stolen my dreams and my childhood with your empty words. And yet I'm one of the lucky ones. People are suffering. People are dying. Entire ecosystems are collapsing. We are in the beginning of a mass extinction, and all you can talk about is money and fairy tales of eternal economic growth. How dare you![5]

Thunberg appealed to the fear of mass extinction in her speech at the UN. She argued that science has been "crystal clear" for more than 30 years, and went on to use quite detailed and technical arguments to argue why urgent political action was required:

> The popular idea of cutting our emissions in half in 10 years only gives us a 50% chance of staying below 1.5 degrees [Celsius], and the risk of setting off irreversible chain reactions beyond human control. Fifty percent may be acceptable to you. But those numbers do not include tipping points, most feedback loops, additional warming hidden by toxic air pollution or the aspects of equity and climate justice. They also rely on my generation sucking hundreds of billions of tons of your CO2 out of the air with technologies that barely exist. So, a 50% risk is simply not acceptable to us — we who have to live with the consequences.

The quite detailed line of argument that Thunberg here used reveals an inherent rhetorical challenge for anyone who wants to appeal to the fear of global warming. As scary as it may seem, the felt fear of climate change may be hard to perceive. It is not as imminent as the instant lack of energy or fuel or the fear of unemployment. The challenge for Thunberg is that the fear she appeals to does not have an immediate object that is as easy to spot as the price of oil. It is much easier to operationalize politics based on the fear that the price of oil or gold may go down or up. The political and rhetorical importance of numbers that the audience immediately feels the effect of became evident to us during the corona pandemic: The display of continuously updated infection rates and death rates provided fertile ground for politicians who wanted to appear vigorous in the face of a crisis. The numbers were "crystal clear" and literally cried for strenuous and efficient action. For a politician who wants to respond to the climate crisis, things are a bit more complicated: The object of fear easily becomes more distant, although there are a few concretes, like the rise in sea level, and the rise in temperatures.

It must be noted though, with a certain sense of irony, that what we once hoped for has now become our deepest fear: Where oil used to be considered the fountain of success and progress, it now denotes our fear for the future. In other words, the object of fear has changed. The public audience is left with a dilemma, or a paradox, if you like. If the world is no longer limitless and open for human dominion, what should we do next? Should we retreat? Whatever comes, we need to prioritize between competing fears. This is the rhetorical challenge every leader faces.

FEAR IN THE ERA OF OIL

Our interest in this book is to describe the ongoing energy crisis and its different developments by analysing a variety of different speeches. We hope to offer pointers on what it may imply to appeal to fear in a well-founded and constructive manner. Our story starts in the year 1973, at the break of the energy crisis emerging from the Yom Kippur war. Two years prior to that war, in 1971, US President Richard Nixon took measures to terminate the deal that the US dollar should be converted to gold, which increased the political and economic importance of oil. The concept of connecting a national currency to the price of gold was known as the so-called Bretton Woods system of monetary management, in which the US and some other major economies agreed to an obligation of adopting a monetary policy that tied their national currencies to gold and the ability of the International Monetary Fund (IMF) to handle temporary imbalances of payments. The aim was to secure global cooperation and prevent the competitive devaluation of national currencies. The fear underlying the whole Bretton Woods system was the fear of repeating the Great Depression. In the 1920s and 30 s, people did not risk investing money because states were acting in an unpredictable way. The Bretton Woods rule sought to hinder too much volatility for developing markets.

When President Nixon in August 1971 issued an executive order that made the dollar inconvertible to gold directly, except on the open market, the dollar then became a floating currency. Gradually the price of oil became a decisive determinator for the currency. It is from this perspective one must understand why former US president Obama was so eager to take credit for the fact that the United States was producing more oil at the end of his presidency than at the beginning. In fact, oil production grew by 88% during Obama's two terms. It revealed Obama's basic fear at the time, not fear of climate change, but the fear that the United States would not be self-supplied with oil.

Speaking in November 2018 the former president Obama reminded the audience at a gala for Rice University's Baker Institute in Houston, Texas that "we are in oil country and we need American energy." He also pointed out that although "you wouldn't always know it, but it went up every year I was president." With a sense of pride, he ended his speech by proclaiming that the whole buzz that "suddenly America's like the biggest oil producer and the biggest gas that was me, people."[6]

Interestingly, there is a recognizable line of thought here, from Jimmy Carter's speech in 1979 and Obama's post-presidential reminder that he secured the US as the world's biggest oil and gas producer. Perhaps it is fair to say that Obama, speaking in oil-land in Texas in 2018, when Donald Trump was President, was less concerned with the apocalyptic fears of global warming, and more concerned with the current political agenda: Obama wanted to emphasize that it was during the watch of a Democratic President that the United States became self-supplied with oil and fulfilled Carter's political ambition. Obama's speech may therefore be interpreted as an attempt to challenge Donald Trump's rhetoric of making America great again. Obama's fear was obviously that Donald Trump would take credit for the rise in oil production.

How should a speaker appeal to fear in the era of oil? Faced with a host of fears, some more imminent than others, the leader who speaks needs to calibrate the delicate balance of prioritizing which fear(s) appeal to— apocalyptic, political, or private fear. Should the fear of running out of oil and the fear of unemployment take prominence over the fear of global warming, which poses a threat to humanity? The dilemma for Obama and other leaders of state is how to speak of two fears at the same time. The problem is how to choose between two competing fears, the fear of running out of energy to grease the economic system and the fear of global warming that may lead to human extinction. The challenge for any leader is to compose a well-founded and persuasive appeal. Considering what is really at stake, the speaker needs to point out the fear that is most worthy of the listeners' attention right here and right now. An additional fear in a liberal democracy is that the speaker and her message could be rejected. You cannot simply instruct people to obey your command. You need to convince your listeners that the fear that governs and directs your decisions should have the same persuasive power over others.

Almost 50 years have passed since 1973. Perhaps we are about to see an end to the era of fossil fuel? In May 2021 the International Energy Agency (IEA) delivered a sort of executioner speech, declaring an end to the era of oil.[7] Basically, they are saying that there is no point in going west anymore. Following the 2021 annual global energy review a report on Net Zero emission by the year 2050 claimed that there is no need to look for new sources of fossil fuel, like oil or gas reserves:

> Building on the IEA's unrivalled energy modelling tools and expertise, the Roadmap sets out more than 400 milestones to guide the global journey to net zero by 2050. These include, from today, no investment in new fossil fuel supply projects, and no further final investment decisions for new unabated coal plants. By 2035, there are no sales of new internal combustion engine passenger cars, and by 2040, the global electricity sector has already reached net-zero emissions. (IEA Press Release, based on Net Zero 2050 report)[8]

This is obviously a dramatic statement from the IEA. Possibly it may even alter our hierarchies of fear. One thing is the fear of the long-term effects of climate change, but for business leaders around the world bound to industries dependent on fossil fuel, we may imagine that another fear becomes even more prominent: What if I and my company are left at the station when the green economy takes off?

The shifting hierarchies of fear as we approach what may be the end of the fossil era play out on a judicial level as well. On May 26, 2021, climate change activists won a major legal victory against oil giant Royal Dutch Shell. A Dutch court ruled that the energy company must reduce its greenhouse gas emissions by 45% by the year 2030, based on 2019 levels. The ruling, in this case, is important because it may set a precedent for similar lawsuits against big oil companies operating internationally.

Sara Shaw, a representative from Friends of the Earth International, proclaimed that "our hope is that this verdict will trigger a wave of climate litigation against big polluters, to force them to stop extracting and burning fossil fuels."[9] It is probably too early to tell if the sun has set on the era of fossil fuel, but for those who still look west for a promising horizon of limitless opportunities, they might discover something else than the black gold.

Two Stories in One—Towards a Rhetoric of Fear

"Be fearless," is the creed of any personal trainer or mental coach who wants to make a living for herself. Our claim, however, is that the leader who faces a crisis needs to appeal to fear in an adequate way in order to appear credible and persuasive. There are obviously problems with appealing to fear. Our simple claim is that the unfolding reality of a crisis demands that we speak into fear: Since 1973 much of the politics in the world, and particularly the Western world, have been fuelled by the fear of running out of oil. Over the last couple of decades, this fear has been mixed with another fear, the fear of global warming caused by the intensive use of fossil energy. In this book, we want to explore the political and rhetorical dilemmas of this era. It may seem pretentious to name the time after 1973 the era of fear. But as we have shown, it makes sense in a certain way. After 1973, the world has been in a constant struggle to secure enough energy, simultaneously dealing with the underlying fear that we might run out of energy.

By moulding the two stories together, the typology of three fears and the story of the ongoing energy and climate crisis, we hope to show how an appeal to fear may serve a constructive purpose in a crisis. By "constructive" we here refer to the rhetorical effect and how it may be possible to manage fear by doing things with words. With this book, we hope to tell the story of why being led by fear is sometimes a bare necessity. In drawing out the elements of a rhetoric of fear, we do not aim to offer a manual for demagogic rhetoric. Rather, we want to discuss what it takes to make an adequate appeal to fear in different situations, and how to make that appeal appear constructive or useful for a particular purpose.

Faced with fear, the leader who wants to speak with authority needs to sort out the stories, symbols, and metaphors that could bear through a crisis. But what strategies could a leader choose when fear rises? One possibility would be to show expediency and vigour by taking decisions.

Another course of action would be to use the opportunity to turn down, or challenge already existing opposition. A sly, and morally questionable strategy would be to point the audience in the direction of one or more potential scapegoats. Thomas Hobbes finds that politics has to do with making people do what you want them to do. The rhetorical challenge implicit in such an approach to politics is how you make something not just credible, but plausible and probable—even trustworthy.

Ultimately, the appeal to fear may be very effective. The presence of fear creates a large range of rhetorical opportunities. If the speaker knows that the audience is afraid, the options are many. Obviously, the public desire for safety provides fertile ground for more ambitious and restrictive policies by the government and other ruling bodies. In the following, we want to evaluate such appeals to fear critically and constructively.

NOTES

1. Jimmy Carter's "crisis of confidence"-speech on July 15, 1979: https://www.americanrhetoric.com/speeches/jimmycartercrisisofconfidence.htm.
2. Jimmy Carter's "crisis of confidence"-speech on July 15, 1979: https://www.americanrhetoric.com/speeches/jimmycartercrisisofconfidence.htm.
3. President George H. W. Bush's speech on August 8, 1990 responding to Iraq's invasion of Kuwait: https://millercenter.org/the-presidency/presidential-speeches/august-8-1990-address-iraqs-invasion-kuwait.
4. For an account of the timeline on oil dependence and US foreign policy: https://www.cfr.org/timeline/oil-dependence-and-us-foreign-policy.
5. Greta Thunberg's speech at the UN climate summit 2019, the "How dare you?"-speech: https://www.npr.org/2019/09/23/763452863/transcript-greta-thunbergs-speech-at-the-u-n-climate-action-summit?t=1588582964843.
6. Barack Obama's speech on the increase in US oil production—"that was me, people" in November 2018 in Houston, Texas: https://apnews.com/article/5dfbc1aa17701ae219239caad0bfefb2.
7. Global energy review IEA 2021: https://www.iea.org/reports/global-energy-review-2021.
8. Net Zero 2050: https://www.iea.org/reports/net-zero-by-2050.
9. Dutch verdict against Royal Dutch Shell on May 26, 2021: https://www.npr.org/2021/05/26/1000475878/in-landmark-case-dutch-court-orders-shell-to-cut-its-carbon-emissions-faster?t=1623139984571 and https://www.reuters.com/business/energy/dutch-court-rule-case-targeting-shells-climate-strategy-2021-05-25/.

BIBLIOGRAPHY

Aristotle: *Rhetoric*. Mineola, New York: Dover, 2004.

Blair, John M.: *The Control of Oil*. New York: Pantheon Books, 1976.

Blake, J.: "Overcoming the 'value-action gap' in environmental policy: Tensions between national policy and local experience." In *Local Environment*, *4*(3), 257–278, 1999.

Cantrill, J. G., & Oravec, C.: *The Symbolic Earth: Discourse and Our Creation of the Environment*. University Press of Kentucky, 1996.

Ceccarelli, L: "Manufactured scientific controversy: Science, rhetoric, and public debate." In *Rhetoric & Public Affairs*, *14*(2), 195–228, 2011.

Cox, J. R.: "The die is cast: Topical and ontological dimensions of the locus of the irreparable." *Quarterly Journal of Speech*, *68*(3), 227–239, 1982.

Dryzek, J. S., & Lo, A. Y.: "Reason and rhetoric in climate communication." In *Environmental Politics*, *24*(1), 1–16, 2015.

Farnsworth, Ward: *Farnsworth's Classical English Rhetoric*. Jaffrey: David R. Godine, 2011.

Fafner, Jørgen: *Tanke og tale. Den retoriske tradition i Vesteuropa*. Copenhagen: C. A. Reitzel, 1978.

Göpel, Maja: *How a New Economic Paradigm and Sustainability Transformations Go Hand in Hand*. Berlin: Wuppertal Institute, 2016.

Hobbes, Thomas: *Leviathan*. Minneapolis: Learner Publishing Group, 2018. First published in 1651.

Hulme, M: *Why We Disagree about Climate Change: Understanding Controversy, Inaction and Opportunity*. Cambridge University Press, 2009.

Kollmuss, A., & Agyeman, J.: "Mind the gap: Why do people act environmentally and what are the barriers to pro-environmental behavior?" In *Environmental Education Research*, *8*(3), 239–260, 2002.

Lausberg, Heinrich et al. (ed.): *Handbook of Literary Rhetoric: A Foundation of Literary Study*. Leiden: Brill, 2002.

Moser, S. C., & Dilling, L.: *Creating a Climate for Change: Communicating Climate Change and Facilitating Social Change*. Cambridge University Press, 2007.

Nilsen, Yngve: *En felles plattform? Norsk oljeindustri og klimadebatten i Norge fram til 1998*. Oslo: Unipub forlag, 2001.

Norheim, Bård & Haga, Joar: *The Four Speeches. Every Leader Has to Know*. London: Palgrave Macmillan (Palgrave Pivot), 2020.

Poortinga, W., Spence, A., Whitmarsh, L., Capstick, S., & Pidgeon, N. F.: "Uncertain climate: An investigation into public scepticism about anthropogenic climate change." In *Global Environmental Change*, *21*(3), 1015–1024, 2011.

Ross, D. G.: *Topic-Driven Environmental Rhetoric*. Routledge, 2017.

Ueding, Gert (ed.): *Historisches Wörterbuch der Rhetorik* (12 volumes). Berlin/New York: Walter de Gruyter, 2015.

United States Federal Trade Commission: *The International Petroleum Cartel*, staff report to the Federal Trade Commission submitted to the Subcommittee on Monopoly of the Select Committee on Small Business, United States Senate, Washington, U. S. Govt. Print. Off., 1952.

Vestrheim, Gjert: *Klassisk retorikk*. Oslo: Dreyers forlag, 2018.

Vickers, Brian: *In Defense of Rhetoric*. Cambridge: Clarendon Press, 1988.

Yukl, Gary: *Leadership in Organizations* (8th edition). New Jersey: Pearson, 2013.

CHAPTER 3

Apocalyptic Fear

Abstract This chapter examines *apocalyptic* fear in more depth. Apocalyptic fear is the most dramatic fear, the sort of fear that appears to threaten our very existence. It is the fear that nature may be collapsing, and that the world is coming to an end. In this chapter, we analyse speeches from a wide variety of leaders, like Mohammed Nasheed, Angela Merkel, Ronald Reagan, Gro Harlem Brundtland, Greta Thunberg, Prince Abdul Aziz bin Salman, and Abdalla Salem El-Badri. The chapter emphasizes the need to create a sense of urgency when appealing to fear and underlines that a leader needs to help people make choices by calling upon a future vision and addressing your rhetorical adversary.

Keywords Apocalyptic fear · The Doomsday Clock · Rhetorical adversary · Executioner speech · Climate change · Nuclear threat · The corona pandemic · Sustainable development · Evil Empire-speech · Chernobyl · Fukushima

The Doomsday Clock

Every year in January the so-called Doomsday Clock is published by the members of the Bulletin of the Atomic Scientists. The clock serves as a metaphor for threats to humanity and portrays the hypothetical global

© The Author(s), under exclusive license to Springer Nature
Switzerland AG 2022
B. Norheim and J. Haga, *The Three Fears Every Leader Has to Know*,
https://doi.org/10.1007/978-3-031-08984-8_3

catastrophe as midnight. The number of minutes or seconds to midnight represents the stance of the world: How close are we to a wide-ranging, worldwide disaster, which would inflict irrevocable harm to humanity?

The key factors setting the time each year are nuclear risk and climate change. Back in 1947, the clock's original setting was seven minutes to midnight, and it has been adjusted several times back and forward since. In 1991, the clock was set at its most optimistic time, 17 min before midnight. The closest calls so far were in January 2020 and January 2021, when the clock was set at 100 s to midnight. Even in January 2022, the Doomsday Clock remained at 100 s to midnight.[1]

The annual publication of the Doomsday Clock is a classic example of what it means to appeal to fear, and more precisely, *apocalyptic* fear, the fear of human extinction. Appealing to apocalyptic fear means proclaiming that the end of times, as we know it, maybe drawing near. The Doomsday clock has therefore become a recognized metaphor around the globe. It plays with the ancient idea of Doomsday, Armageddon, or the Final Day of Judgement, which is a well-established notion in many cultures. The image of the clock is also an effective symbol. For one, the audience is set to believe in the accuracy of the scientists' judgement of the fluctuating fears of our time. Secondly, as the Doomsday clock sets a time, it leaves you with the feeling that the portrayed threat is something that follows with necessity and the preciseness of a fine-tuned clockwork. Thirdly, the image of Midnight is a universally accepted metaphor for the emergence of darkness and potentially evil forces.

Unsurprisingly, the Doomsday clock also has its critics. Some would claim that it is unhelpful and less constructive to put humanity on high alert in this manner and that it is more likely to contribute to public paralysis. The clock becomes like the shepherd boy in Aesop's fable who cried "wolf!" Twice, the villagers responded to his false alarm and came to his rescue. The third time, when the wolf came, the townspeople refused to believe the boy's alarming cries.[2] Others find that the methodology of the clock is highly disputable and far from objective. Nevertheless, the appeal of the Doomsday clock works. The metaphor strikes. The clock tells a story. It is yet another example of how the appeal to fear implies appealing to a *perceived* fear, not simply a statistically calibrated fear. For the speaker who aims to give an adequate and constructive appeal to fear, it is therefore important to find a striking and persuasive metaphor which both draws on cultural memory and makes a credible account of the matter at hand.

"If Things Go Business
as Usual, We Will Not Live"

On September 22, 2009, the newly elected President of the island state Maldives, Mohamed Nasheed gave a passionate address to the United Nations Climate Summit in New York. He warned the audience that "if things go business as usual, we will not live." Nasheed extended an intense appeal to an imminent fear. He warned that the world, as we know it, is about to become inhabitable. He stated bluntly that people in the Maldives will die, "our country will not exist." What Nasheed here described was an emerging apocalyptic threat. Suffering the impact of the Arctic polar caps melting and the waters warming up, the Maldives are threatened by rising sea levels, extreme weather, and coral bleaching. Responding to that threat, Nasheed announced that:

> It is now in all of our national interest to jump first and jump far. That is why the Maldives, without waiting for the outcome of the Copenhagen summit recently announced its intention to become carbon neutral by 2020.[3]

Further, Nasheed encouraged the assembled world leaders to seize "the historic opportunity," at the Climate change summit in Copenhagen in December of the same year. The President promised that the Maldives would "lead by example," but he also exhorted other world leaders to "discard those habits that have led to twenty years of complacency and broken promises on climate change." Speaking with an intense sense of urgency, Nasheed extended a final appeal to the audience, envisioning the implications of the threat that lay before his eyes:

> Please, ladies and gentlemen, we did not do any of these things, but if things go business as usual, we will not live. We will die. Our country will not exist. We cannot come out from Copenhagen as failures. We cannot make Copenhagen a pact for suicide.

It is obvious that President Nasheed appealed to apocalyptic fear, the fear that our world may be annihilated and that human beings may be facing extinction. A few months later, on December 14, Nasheed addressed the Climate Change Meeting in Copenhagen. He then used his own personal narrative, his *ethos*, to craft another intense and persuasive appeal. This speech also appealed to fear, but Nasheed simultaneously urged the world to commit to climate action in the light of hope.

Where the speech from September had elements of an executioner speech, with Nasheed offering a harsh verdict of complacent world leaders, the speech in Copenhagen was more of a classical opening speech. The former President of the Maldives named reality to envision a future cause that he urged the audience to commit to. In his attempt to present a persuasive message, Nasheed used his own experience of imprisonment when the Maldives was a totalitarian regime. He described how the four years in solitary confinement sometimes made him doubt the purpose of the fight for freedom and democracy. But "in spite of the odds, we refused to give up hope," the President encouraged the Copenhagen audience.

In a final comparison, between the story of fighting for freedom and democracy in the Maldives and the apocalyptic challenge that the globe is facing, Nasheed maintained that although he and his comrades won the battle for democracy in the Maldives, the path to democracy was not "straight-forward." Similarly, the fight for climate justice also offers difficult and bumpy terrain, Nasheed argued:

> We are here to save our planet from the silent, patient and invisible enemy that is climate change. And just as there were doubters in the Maldives, so there are doubters in Copenhagen. There are those who tell us that solving climate change is impossible. There are those who tell us taking radical action is too difficult. There are those who tell us to give up hope. Well, I am here to tell you that we refuse to give up hope. We refuse to be quiet. We refuse to believe that a better world isn't possible.[4]

A Renaissance for Apocalyptic Communication?

The climate crisis and even the corona pandemic have offered a sort of renaissance for apocalyptic communication. Our current perception of reality has made it easier for those who warn us that the world, our entire *cosmos*, might be falling apart. We live in a fertile rhetorical climate for anyone who wants to proclaim that doomsday is not a metaphor for a distant future, but an unfolding reality here and now. Environmental prophets like Greta Thunberg who warn of an apocalypse now, are no longer a laughingstock, but make a political impact. In a time where the appeal to fear, seems both relevant and well-founded, the audience usually expects two alternative courses of action, either an appeal to a dramatic change in behaviour, like a revolution, or some sort of medicine that may fix the problem, like a vaccine or a technical solution to the energy problem.

To get a better hold of what sort of fear apocalyptic fear is, we need to consider the good, the bad, and the ugly. Or to be more precise, we need to consider our conception of good and evil. How do you determine what makes something good, and another thing evil? More importantly, what if loving the good even involves fearing or perhaps hating that which is evil? In the Psalms in the Bible, one is constantly reminded that loving the good, implies hating evil. Similarly, the message of the Old Testament prophets implied inducing fear, sometimes even the fear that the world is at "the cliff's edge." Apocalyptic fear is total, and not constrained to one part or aspect of life. It is the fear that you may wake up in a house with no floor. The appeal to apocalyptic fears puts the audience on the election stand, do you want to choose evil or good? It means drawing the audience into a future vision that human existence as we know it may be coming to an end.

Most societies today are reliant on access to energy. Losing power or being cut off energy supply could offer the feeling of apocalyptic fear. An appeal to apocalyptic fear may include envisioning a future where access to energy may be restricted or perhaps even denied. This sort of fear cannot simply be rationalized and subdued. It has to be treated rhetorically. In other words, the ongoing oil and climate crisis is an actual ongoing experience, which needs to be addressed. It is not just a potential crisis. It is an actual crisis. This creates a rhetorical space of opportunity.

What qualifies as apocalyptic fear obviously depends on the situation at hand. Let us take a recent example: The corona pandemic appeared to many as an apocalyptic fear, because it was a plague, and a plague is something that by definition may threaten human extinction, according to our cultural memory. Let us then consider a more distant example, the Second World War. For most the war is a historical memory. To appeal to its fears today, you need to reactivate the memory and argue why fearing the atrocities of the war may be relevant, like maintaining that we have to watch out for the emergence of totalitarian ideologies.

What does the renaissance for apocalyptic communication mean for someone who wants to make a well-founded appeal to fear in the era of the climate and energy crisis? In the 1960s and early 1970s, most people thought energy, whether fossil or not, was like a gold mine. The more you could get access to, the merrier. It was all about securing the accelerating growth of society with enough resources to continue its growth. It was like providing a train with enough coal to accelerate and increase its speed towards a promising future destination. Now, we face the possibility of an apocalyptic climate crisis. We have moved from a techno-optimistic view of energy—and oil in particular—to a more apocalyptic view. However, our old friend techno-optimism is still within arm's reach. After all, many people would prefer a technical solution to the apocalyptic threats of the climate crisis.

HERE, THERE, AND EVERYWHERE—THE FEAR OF A NUCLEAR DISASTER

On Friday, March 11, 2011, a severe nuclear accident occurred at the Fukushima Daiichi Nuclear Power Plant in Japan. The event was caused by an earthquake and the following tsunami. It turned out to be the most severe nuclear accident since the Chernobyl disaster in 1986, being classified along with the Chernobyl catastrophe as Level 7 on the International Nuclear Event Scale. 154.000 people had to be evacuated because of the disaster. In the days following the event, radiation was released into the atmosphere and forced the Japanese government to declare an ever-larger evacuation zone around the plant. The final evacuation zone reached a 20 km radius.

The severity of the Fukushima accident caused political reactions in other countries reliant on nuclear energy. The German Chancellor Angela Merkel spoke to the German Bundestag less than a week after the accident. In her speech, she tried to describe the almost apocalyptic reality, caused by the earthquake and tsunami. She maintained that the catastrophe in Japan had "an almost apocalyptic dimension, and we strive to find the right words." The disaster in Japan, according to Merkel, required a new order of business, or *Tagesordnung* in German. But here followed Merkel's dilemma in her address to the Bundestag: The Chancellor did indeed acknowledge the apocalyptic fear involved when using nuclear power plants, even in Germany. At the same time, she assured the listeners that the plants in Germany were as safe as possible. She remained hesitant to terminate the use of nuclear power plants altogether and presented the audience with the following political challenge:

> Yes, it is true, indeed: Energy in Germany needs to be offered to people at an affordable cost, and we have not solved any problem, if workplaces

are removed to other countries, where the security of the nuclear power plants are no better (than here), perhaps even poorer.

Merkel then returned to the apocalyptic perspective and argued that "the inconceivable events in Japan teach us that something, which all scientific parameters claimed to be impossible, could still happen."[5]

In the rest of her speech, Merkel engaged in a long and rather detailed debate with her political opposition, arguing why an instant moratorium on nuclear power plants would not be a solution to the energy crisis. We still need nuclear energy to bridge the energy gap, until we have enough renewable energy available, the Chancellor maintained. In her speech Merkel was eager to describe the complexity of the political dilemma related to nuclear power plants. On one hand, nuclear power plants in Germany provide a safe source of clean energy, at least compared to coal and oil-driven energy solutions. On the other hand, every nuclear power plant represents a reminder of an imminent apocalyptic threat. They are local Doomsday Clock's and ticking bombs. If it can happen there, it can happen here, and it can happen everywhere. This seems to be the logic of the apocalyptic fear of nuclear disasters. Merkel's speech is an interesting example of how a leader tries to calibrate her appeal to different kinds of fear. On one hand, she appealed to the apocalyptic fear of a nuclear disaster. On the other hand, she appealed to political fear, like the rise in energy prices or unemployment. Probably, the Chancellor tried to name the dilemma and complexity of the problem to make her argument of postponing the moratorium of nuclear energy appear more persuasive.

Later the same year, in June 2011, Merkel once again addressed the Bundestag on the question of nuclear power. She then argued for the decision to phase out nuclear energy by 2022, which she found was "a Herculean task." She exhorted her listeners to "work together on this project to combine future ethical responsibilities with economic success." However, the opposition was not convinced of Merkel's sudden change of heart, and the Greens and the Social Democratic Party representatives criticized Merkel for being late to the party.[6]

1983 AS APOCALYPSE NOW: THE WORLD
ON THE BRINK OF NUCLEAR WAR

It seems like a very long time ago, but in 1983 many people feared that the world was on the brink of nuclear war. During the Northern hemisphere autumn months, the world witnessed several nuclear close calls. One was the false alarm of a satellite early-warning system near Moscow on five incoming foreign missiles on the 26th of September 1983. Luckily, Lieutenant Colonel Stanislav Petrov of the Air Defence Forces refused to treat the threat as legitimate until it could be confirmed by ground radar. Later the same year, NATO military forces carried out a command post exercise, Able Archer 83, simulating a Soviet conventional attack on European NATO forces three days before the start of the exercise.

Tensions rose high and Soviet leaders came to believe that the exercise was a way to cover up NATO preparations for a nuclear first strike. In a state of panic, Soviet leaders sent a telegram to its residences trying to obtain information on NATO preparations for an attack. The problem was that the Able Archer exercise resembled the Soviet timeline estimations of a NATO first strike, which would take seven to ten days to execute after the political decision had been made. Fortunately, Soviet forces stood down after 11 November as the Able Archer exercise ended, and for a while, NATO was unaware of the complete Soviet response until British intelligence asset Oleg Gordievsky later passed on information about the frantic Soviet preparations.[7]

The Soviet response to the Able Archer exercise bears witness to how we often respond to an imminent feeling of apocalyptic fear, particularly when we are already alarmed by previous incidents and a staggering feeling of increasing fears. All in all, the year 1983 really came with a profound apocalyptic flavour. It has later been revealed by the opening of old archives that British officials even drafted an emotional speech for Queen Elizabeth II. The speech was supposed to serve as part of an exercise simulating the outbreak of nuclear war, a sort of an apocalyptic Cold War Scenario. Luckily, one may add, the monarch was never put in a position where she had to rehearse or perform the speech. Most likely, she never even saw the script.[8]

However, the most prominent "apocalyptic speech" of the year 1983 was delivered by American President, Ronald Reagan. On March 8, 1983, the former actor addressed a group of Conservative Christians at the National Association of Evangelicals in Orlando, Florida. The speech was later named the *Evil Empire*-speech. Reagan had given a similar speech less than a year earlier to the British House of Commons. In that speech, he focused on what he found to be the Soviet Union's diabolic political power.

In the Orlando speech Ronald Reagan enacted a sort of American version of Sir Winston Churchill as he appeared and spoke during the first years of the Second World War. Reagan warned against underestimating the sort of power the Soviet Union represented, as the so-called "nuclear freeze proposals" were considered. The President exhorted the audience to pay attention and urged them not to ignore the imminent threat at hand:

> So, in your discussions of the nuclear freeze proposals, I urge you to beware the temptation of pride–the temptation of blithely .. uh .. declaring yourselves above it all and label both sides equally at fault, to ignore the facts of history and the aggressive impulses of an evil empire, to simply call the arms race a giant misunderstanding and thereby remove yourself from the struggle between right and wrong and good and evil.[9]

Ronald Reagan's appeal to consider the arms race as part of a struggle between good and evil bears similarities to Moses' farewell speech in the Old Testament. At the end of his life, upon entering the Promised Land, Moses as the long-time leader of the Israelites set up two alternatives for the people, the way of life and the way of death. He urged them to choose life, so that the Israelites and their children may live. (Deuteronomy 30:19) Similarly, President Reagan contrasted the American way of life with an evil empire.

If you listen carefully to the speech from March 1983, it becomes clear that Reagan wanted to place his audience not merely in the midst of a political crisis, but in a cosmic drama. The American President tried to showcase communism as a version of original sin. Reagan first warned that the crisis of the Western world "exists to the degree in which the West is indifferent to God, the degree to which it collaborates in communism's attempt to make man stand alone without God." Reagan then continued and asserted, quoting Whittaker Chambers:

Marxism-Leninism is actually the second-oldest faith, first proclaimed in the Garden of Eden with the words of temptation, "Ye shall be as gods."

The President proceeded to urge the American nation to rise to the challenge, in what he argued was a spiritual, rather than a material quest for human freedom. Ending with an elevated pastoral tone, in a grand style of speech, Reagan boldly announced, quoting the prophet Isaiah:

The source of our strength in the quest for human freedom is not material, but spiritual. And because it knows no limitation, it must terrify and ultimately triumph over those who would enslave their fellow man. For in the words of Isaiah: "He giveth power to the faint; and to them that have no…might… He increased strength. But they that wait upon the Lord shall renew their strength; they shall mount up with wings as eagles; they shall run, and not be weary." [Applause]

Reagan's appeal is a calibrated mix of apocalyptic fear and a more political fear. The threat Reagan tried to portray was both political and potentially apocalyptic: The Soviet Union was not just a political adversary, but it represented a power that could mean the end of the world, if it was not controlled or defeated, so Reagan argued. We here see how appealing to fear, by adopting vivid metaphorical imagery with cosmic dimensions, enabled the speaker to provide what must have been a persuasive argument for many at the time. The line of argument provided a rational logic for the political purpose of the speech, namely, to increase defence budgets. In retrospect one may argue that the appeal to fear was exaggerated, but the point from a rhetorical perspective is that the speaker made it appear well-founded and in a certain sense rational given the situation at hand.

A few years later, in 1985, British pop artist Sting released a single which served as an indirect critique of Reagan's speech and the appeal to fear during the Cold War era, particularly the doctrine of mutual assured destruction (MAD). The song was called *Russians*. In the song Sting warned against the apocalyptic fear of nuclear destruction, labelled "Oppenheimer's deadly toy." This was a reference to the American physicist Robert Oppenheimer, who was considered "the father of the atomic bomb." Oppenheimer later expressed deep regrets for creating the bomb and said he had intended it to be used for energy use in peacetime. In contrast to the appeal to fear in Reagan's speech, Sting's song tapped into another kind of fear, a sort of private fear, the fear that we may lose ourselves as we race to win a battle of cold war:

> How can I save my little boy from Oppenheimer's deadly toy?
> There is no monopoly on common sense
> On either side of the political fence
> We share the same biology, regardless of ideology
> Believe me when I say to you
> I hope the Russians love their children too
> There is no historical precedent
> To put the words in the mouth of the president?
> There's no such thing as a winnable war[10]

Human beings usually adopt different strategies when faced with death and apocalypse. The ultimate purpose would be to *control* death, but that would in most cases be a failed approach. The next alternative is to seek *safety* in the face of death. Could medicine provide the answer? What about financial solutions? Or do we have to look to philosophy, religion— or even theology? The appeal to fear relates to our current perception of reality. Interestingly, the fear of nuclear war has decreased over the last decades. This is not because the threat itself has been reduced or because the fear is no longer justified. No, the fear of nuclear war has been replaced by other fears in a constantly shifting hierarchy of fears. We know that fear of nuclear disasters influences people's willingness to take risks in terms of savings. The point is that a perceived and increased threat of nuclear war reduces the public's willingness to think in the long term and take an economic risk.[11] In other words, as times change our perception of fear changes. In a global, digital age digital fears are becoming more prominent. In June 2021 it was announced that the US Department of Justice will give ransomware attacks similar priority as terrorist attacks.[12]

YOU CAN ONLY FEAR WHAT YOU ALREADY KNOW, RIGHT?

In his speech on the Evil empire Ronald Reagan crafted an appeal to fear that tapped into the political imaginary of the audience, and the more apocalyptic fear for a future disaster. Both the appeal to a political imaginary, cultural memory, and the appeal to the metaphoric of a future catastrophe drew on a well-established rhetorical legacy in the American context. But what if a fear emerges, that seems incomparable to previous fears, and which sits outside our well-known train of thought. Is it possible to make an audience fear something that appears foreign to their own context? On a banal and intuitive level, one could ask what it would take to make listeners from a tropical climate fear a slippery, icy road. Similarly, one could ask how people living around the Polar circle could be brought to fear the emergence of a devastating heat wave.

Faced with fear, we tend to overreact. The challenge for a leader during a crisis where fear is imminent is to sort out what piece of information represents noise and what sort of information should be read as a signal to act on. The challenge with a crisis is not necessarily the crisis itself, but the fear that the crisis leaves us with. When the crisis is over, we are often prone to over-produce systems that are supposed to avoid a similar crisis in the future. This could easily lead us to create more vulnerable systems, because we tend to believe that failure is the product of poor forecasting. However, that is not necessarily the case. We tend to forget that we fear the unpredictable because it is not forecastable. Nassim Nicholas Taleb has described an unpredictable and unexpected future event with potentially severe consequences as a Black Swan incident. Black swan events are characterized by their extreme rarity and severe impact. Ironically, Taleb mourns, a whole host of experts usually insist that they were obvious in hindsight.[13]

OUR COMMON FUTURE, OUR COMMON APOCALYPSE

The ongoing climate and energy crisis is a constant reminder of the fact that we live in a highly globalized world. The global scale of the climate crisis is potentially both fear-provoking and hope-generating. How should a speaker who wants to speak about the potential fears of globalization and climate crisis craft her speech? Let us rewind to the mid-1980s when the climate crisis started to rise high on the political agenda around the globe. The report, *Our Common Future*, was published in October 1987 by the United Nations. It was also known as *the Brundtland Report*, named after former Norwegian prime minister Gro Harlem Brundt-land, who had been chairing the World Commission on Environment and Development (WCED). The report advocated multilateralism and emphasized the interdependence of nations on the path to sustainable development.[14]

The aim of *Our Common Future* was to place environmental issues on the political agenda, underlining that it was of paramount importance to discuss environmental challenges and developmental challenges as one single issue. The report focused on poverty reduction, gender equality, and wealth redistribution as key factors in launching a strategy for environmental conservation. The report also acknowledged the environmental limits to economic growth in the industrial world.

The Brundtland report claimed that poverty reduces sustainability and may accelerate environmental pressures. In other words, there is a need to balance between economy and ecology. The report and the work of the Commission sparked the initiative to host the 1992 Earth Summit in Rio de Janeiro and the adoption of Agenda 21, the Rio Declaration and the establishment of the Commission on Sustainable Development. A frequently quoted phrase from the report is the definition of sustainable development: "development that meets the needs of the present without compromising the ability of future generations to meet their own needs." Nowadays, the 17 sustainable development goals (SDG) have become instrumental both in business and politics.[15]

To Brundtland the concept "sustainable development," was "a broad concept for social and economic progress." It was wired to fight poverty as a prime suspect of environmental deterioration. One may of course ask if the Brundtland commission's take on development and growth displayed a rather utopian definition of sustainability. Anyhow, the commission's report was very clear in identifying the situation in the late 1980s as a crisis. The report argued that present development patterns had to change and that threats to the environment were becoming "global in scope and devastating in scale":

> The survival of this planet requires that we act now! The Commission came out equally convinced that the necessary changes are also possible. Our report is not a prophecy of doom, but a positive vision of the future.[16]

The commission was mainly concerned with the protection of the ozone layer, but it was also much concerned with how global warming was expected "to change agricultural and settlement patterns and flood seaports." In her address to the UN General Assembly in 1987 prime minister Brundtland tried to appeal to the audience to voluntarily commit themselves to "a positive vision of the future." She was reluctant to apply an open appeal to fear. Brundtland advocated "a positive vision of the future," a belief that "the necessary changes are also possible." The commission boldly proclaimed that "our common concerns for the future can create a momentum of change."

If we examine Brundtland's speech carefully, we realize that there was no explicit appeal to fear, but the Norwegian prime minister appealed to fear in a rather indirect and implicit manner. It followed from her naming of reality. We see this line of thought in how Brundtland argued that there was no need to dwell on "the familiar catalogue of environmental deterioration." Rather, the medicine prescribed was "strengthening commodity markets," and abolishing "restrictive trade prices." The report even promoted the "integration of environment and economics into decision-making at all levels."

It is worth paying attention to how Brundtland extended a politically laden appeal to global unity. She urged the audience to commit with loyalty to the UN Secretary General. He needed "our total support," and Brundtland argued that "a very special role is to be played by our Secretary General." We see how Brundtland's speech promoted a positive view on globalization, maintaining that "time has come to move forward towards a true revival of multilateralism." Brundtland imagined an interaction between all key players, like NGOs, trade unions, and women, based on "exchange of information, creative dialogue, and inspiration." Later the same day, Brundtland gave the James Marshall Memorial Lecture. Here she appealed more explicitly to fear by pointing out that "over three years we looked into the future and found that so many current human activities are blind alleys down which lie increased poverty and decreased options for future generations."

Fast forward 30 years and it seems like the Brundtland report's global optimism has been replaced with cosmic pessimism. The doomsday prophets have moved centre stage. As we already noted in the previous chapter, Swedish climate activist, Greta Thunberg, addressed the United Nations Climate Summit in September 2019 in New York. It may not be fair to compare the two speeches, as Thunberg spoke in another capacity than Brundtland. Still, the difference in rhetoric is noticeable. Thunberg took on the role of the doomsday prophet, claiming that the adult leaders of the world had stolen her dreams and her childhood with empty words. She went on to proclaim:

People are suffering. People are dying. Entire ecosystems are collapsing. We are in the beginning of a mass extinction, and all you can talk about is money and fairy tales of eternal economic growth. How dare you![17]

Gro Harlem Brundtland's appeal to the UN back in 1987 was presented in a hopeful tone. So was President Mohammed Nasheed's speech in Copenhagen in December 2009. Why do different speakers take on different roles or characters as they address similar threats and fears? After all, the challenge of climate change presented an apocalyptic threat to the audience, even in 1987, but perhaps not with the same imminent urgency as in 2009 and 2019. One thing is for sure, the three leaders in question were positioned differently when they addressed climate change. Brundtland was the prime minister of an oil-producing country commissioned to write a report on sustainability. Her speech was a sort of opening speech, where Brundtland appealed to a greater, global "we" and change in mentality. Nasheed spoke as the newly elected head of state of an island state suffering the immediate consequences of climate change. He shifted between appealing to fear and hope as he spoke to other global leaders. Thunberg, on the other hand, positioned herself as an outsider, accusing "you," the adult, global leaders of stealing her childhood. Her speech was presented as an executioner speech, where she accused world leaders of moral bankruptcy.

NAVIGATING CONFLICTING FEARS

When a threat emerges, there are often conflicting fears at play. One typical example is the fear of global warming on one hand, and the fear of losing jobs and economic resources on the other hand. How do politicians address those conflicting fears? How do you calibrate the appeal to apocalyptic fear and political fear simultaneously? It is particularly interesting to examine how politicians who lead countries that have built their wealth and welfare on producing oil and gas appeal to an often conflicting set of fears. In February 2020, the Kingdom of Saudi Arabia hosted the International Carbon Capture Utilization and Storage (ICCUS) Conference, in its capacity as a prominent member of *OPEC*. OPEC is short for *The Organization of the Petroleum Exporting Countries*. In Chapter 2 we saw how the organization has had a major influence on global oil prices. With its headquarters in Vienna, Austria, the 13 member countries account for approximately 40% of global oil production and hold around

80% of the world's known oil reserves. At the 2020 conference, Saudi Arabia's Minister of Energy, HRH Prince Abdul Aziz bin Salman, spoke to address the issue of global warming and the fears it causes. He started his speech by openly acknowledging that "the task of reducing global greenhouse gas emissions is challenging." In other words, he identified a crisis and acknowledged the presence of a threat.

However, bin Salman quickly moved on to emphasize that although "alternative energy sources are expanding, the world continues to rely upon fossil fuels for the overwhelming share of its overall energy needs." It seems obvious that the Saudi Prince tried to manoeuvre between two conflicting fears. We have looked at how a speaker who is able to name reality in a convincing manner, is usually better positioned to present a credible and attractive path towards the future. The prince tried to name reality by emphasizing that the situation will "not change for many decades to come." In other words, simply stopping oil and gas production is not an option, at least not in bin Salman's portrait of reality.

In the next section of the speech bin Salman used the Brundtland report's main argument to his advantage. He connected the idea of development and sustainability, which was key in the former UN report, emphasizing that:

> Given that energy is a key input for both economic and social development, we also need to develop and deploy energy solutions that effectively address the problem of greenhouse gas emissions while also powering prosperity now and in the future.

The final remark—"now and in the future"—almost sounds like an echo of the well-known definition of sustainable development in the *Our Common Future* by the Brundtland commission: Sustainable development is "development that meets the needs of the present without compromising the ability of future generations to meet their own needs." The Prince ended his speech by quoting former US President Teddy Roosevelt in arguing for taking on the Saudi Kingdom's preferred technical solution to combat climate change, namely *CCUS*—Carbon Capture, Utilization, and Storage. With Roosevelt, bin Salman reminded the audience that "'nothing in the world is worth having or worth doing unless it means effort, pain, (and) difficulty.'"[18]

For a speaker who tries to navigate conflicting fears, naming reality is key. This is particularly important if the fear you may want to downplay is almost impossible to ignore, like global warming. Many, particularly in a Western context, would probably question the motifs and sincerity of Bin Salman in his address. The prince's speech is an evident example of how a speaker strives to reorder the hierarchy of fears. He first addressed apocalyptic fear (T0), and later argued, at least indirectly, why political fear (T1) should take prominence as the more urgent fear. The Minister did indeed speak of the possible fear of human extinction through global warming, but he contrasted that fear with the fear that civilization may fall apart if we stop producing oil. After all, the prince argued, energy is the one thing that enables a continued fight against poverty and unemployment. The technical solution, CCUS—Carbon Capture, Utilization, and Storage became the decisive *logos*-argument in the rhetorical calibration between the two fears.

Let us consider a similar rhetorical dilemma at a time when the financial crisis took hold of world politics and finances. Then OPEC Secretary General, HE Abdalla Salem El-Badri, spoke at the 10th International Oil Summit in Paris at the beginning of April 2009. He asked, "what does the future hold for the oil industry?" Like the Saudi Prince in 2020, El-Badri started by naming reality. The Secretary General described the effects of the financial crisis, and the great fall in oil prices at length. At the end of the speech, El-Badri used the same sort of argument that Prince bin Salman did, substituting the impact of one fear, by highlighting another fear, namely the fear of energy deficit and prosperity decrease and loss of development if fossil fuels were not at "the heart of meeting global energy needs for the foreseeable future."[19]

El-Badri also appealed to how investment in the oil industry would "attract and retain much-needed manpower." Finally, the OPEC Secretary General deducted the sustainable development argument from the Brundtland commission and used it for his own rhetorical purposes, claiming that "protecting the environment should be about enhancing the future for generations to come, not promoting specific political agendas." We see in this speech an appeal to the techno-optimism following the Enlightenment era and the industrial revolution. It is the idea of human dominion over nature as a means to extract the necessary resources for continued growth.

In times of crisis, the feeling of apocalypse could pop up in many ways. Something as simple as being cut off power, could create a slightly apocalyptic feeling. In our modern world one may feel unprotected when the access to energy is restricted or denied. It is almost like being kept away from the water supply. It feels like you are cut off from the opportunity to participate in progress. From a rhetorical perspective, the crucial question is this: Who becomes a leader in the face of an apocalyptic threat? Is it the guy at the gas station telling you when the next reserve of fuel will arrive, or perhaps the city mayor who persuasively tells you how they will fix the water supply?

As always, the speaker who can give an adequate account of reality is more likely to be trusted and attract followers. When a major catastrophe strikes, the audience is faced with an urgent dilemma, who should we turn to, who should we trust? Even for the leader in charge, it is a question of trust: To which extent should I trust my instincts and intuition, and to which extent should I seek the advice of others? Looking at the drama from the outside, one may simply ask, who becomes a leader in the face of death? Who becomes a sage, a poet, or even a prophet when the fear of death and disaster is lurking around every corner?

Notes

1. For more on the Doomsday Clock, cf: https://thebulletin.org/doomsday-clock/.
2. Aesop's fables and "the boy who cried wolf": https://fablesofaesop.com/the-boy-who-cried-wolf.html.
3. President Mohammed Nasheed of the Maldives speaking at the UN Global Climate Summit, 22nd of September 2009: "Our country will no longer exist": https://www.youtube.com/watch?v=QLmP40gYH7c and http://english.cctv.com/20090923/102048.shtml.
4. President Mohammed Nasheed of the Maldives speaking at the Copenhagen Klimaforum 09 in December 2009: https://presidency.gov.mv/Press/Article/1781.
5. Angela Merkel's speech on March 17, 2011 to the Bundestag (video): https://www.c-span.org/video/?298681-1/german-chancellor-angela-merkel-speech-bundestag-nuclear-power. Transcript in German of the March 17, 2011 speech. https://archiv.bundesregierung.de/archiv-de/regierungserklaerung-der-bundeskanzlerin-angela-merkel-zur-aktuellen-lage-in-japan-mitschrift--1122342 (authors' translation from the German original).
6. Angels Merkel's speech to the Bundestag in June 2011: https://www.dw.com/en/merkel-faces-opposition-eye-rolling-amid-plea-for-nuclear-phaseout/a-15143236 and https://www.nytimes.com/2011/06/10/world/europe/10iht-germany10.html.

7. Andrew, Christopher & Gordievsky, Oleg: *Comrade Kryuchkov's Instructions: Top Secret Files on KGB Foreign Operations, 1975–1985*. Stanford, CA: Stanford University Press, 1993. Cf also: Union of Concerned Scientists: *Close Call with Nuclear Weapons*. https://www.ucsusa.org/sites/default/files/attach/2015/04/Close%20Calls%20with%20Nuclear%20Weapons.pdf.

8. The speech that was never given by the Queen of England in 1983: https://www.smh.com.au/world/the-queens-1983-nuclear-war-speech-that-was-never-given-20130801-2r0n7.html.

9. President Ronald Reagan's speech to the National Association of Evangelicals on March 8, 1983, transcript, and video: http://voicesofdemocracy.umd.edu/reagan-evil-empire-speech-text/ and https://www.youtube.com/watch?v=FcSm-KAEFFA. Cf. also Ronald Reagan's speech to House of Commons in June 1982, the thematic preamble to the Evil Empire Speech: https://sourcebooks.fordham.edu/mod/1982reagan1.asp. Cf also: Schweizer, Peter: *Victory: The Reagan Administration's Secret Strategy That Hastened the Collapse of the Soviet Union*. New York: The Atlantic Monthly Press, 1994.

10. Sting: "Russians." The song was released on the album: *The Dream of the Blue Turtles* (1985).

11. Slemrod, Joel: "Saving and the fear of nuclear war." In *The Journal of Conflict Resolution*, 30(3), 403–419, September 1986.

12. US government to give ransomware attacks same attention as terrorism: https://www.reuters.com/technology/exclusive-us-give-ransomware-hacks-similar-priority-terrorism-official-says-2021-06-03/.

13. Taleb, Nassim Nicholas: *The Black Swan*. New York: Random House, 2010 and Taleb, Nassim Nicholas: *Antifragile: Things that Gain from Disorder*. New York: Random House, 2014.

14. World Commission on Environment and Development: *Our Common Future*. Oxford: Oxford University Press, 1987.

15. Cf the presentation of the sustainable development goals at this UN website, https://sdgs.un.org/goals.

16. Link to selected speeches from the Brundtland commission: https://idl-bnc-idrc.dspacedirect.org/handle/10625/20579.

17. Greta Thunberg's speech at the UN climate summit in 2019, the "How dare you?"-speech: https://www.npr.org/2019/09/23/763452863/transcript-greta-thunbergs-speech-at-the-u-n-climate-action-summit?t=1588582964843.

18. Saudi Arabia's Minister of Energy, HRH Prince Abdul Aziz bin Salman's speech in 2020: https://www.opec.org/opec_web/en/press_room/5850.htm.

19. OPEC Secretary General HE Abdalla Salem El-Badri's speech in Paris on April 2nd, 2009: https://www.opec.org/opec_web/en/press_room/809.htm.

BIBLIOGRAPHY

Andrew, Christopher & Gordievsky, Oleg: *Comrade Kryuchkov's Instructions: Top Secret Files on KGB Foreign Operations, 1975–1985.* Stanford, CA: Stanford University Press, 1993.

Aristotle: *Rhetoric.* Mineola, New York: Dover, 2004.

Barr, S., & Gilg, A. W. "A conceptual framework for understanding and analyzing attitudes towards environmental behaviour." *Geografiska Annaler: Series B, Human Geography, 89*(4), 361–379, 2007.

Dryzek, J. S., & Lo, A. Y. "Reason and rhetoric in climate communication." In *Environmental Politics, 24*(1), 1–16, 2015.

Farnsworth, Ward: *Farnsworth's Classical English Rhetoric.* Jaffrey: David R. Godine, 2011.

Fafner, Jørgen: *Tanke og tale. Den retoriske tradition i Vesteuropa.* Copenhagen: C. A. Reitzel, 1978.

Heifetz, Ronald A.: *Leadership without Easy Answers.* Cambridge, MA: Belknap Press of Harvard University Press, 1994.

Hulme, M. *Why We Disagree about Climate Change: Understanding Controversy, Inaction and Opportunity.* Cambridge University Press, 2009.

Humes, James C: *The Sir Winston Method. Five Secrets of Speaking the Language of Leadership.* New York: William Morrow & Company, 1991.

Kollmuss, A., & Agyeman, J. "Mind the gap: Why do people act environmentally and what are the barriers to pro-environmental behavior?" *Environmental Education Research, 8*(3), 239–260, 2002.

Lamb, W. F., Mattioli, G., Levi, S., Roberts, J. T., Capstick, S., Creutzig, F., Minx, J. C., Müller-Hansen, F., Culhane, T., & Steinberger, J. K. "Discourses of climate delay." In *Global Sustainability,* 2020.

Lausberg, Heinrich, et al. (ed.): *Handbook of Literary Rhetoric: A Foundation of Literary Study.* Leiden: Brill, 2002.

Oreskes, N., & Conway, E. M: *Merchants of Doubt: How a Handful of Scientists Obscured the Truth on Issues from Tobacco Smoke to Global Warming.* Bloomsbury Publishing USA, 2010.

Ross, D. G.: *Topic-Driven Environmental Rhetoric.* Routledge, 2017.

Schweizer, Peter: *Victory: The Reagan Administration's Secret Strategy That Hastened the Collapse of the Soviet Union* New York: The Atlantic Monthly Press, 1994.

Slemrod, Joel: "Saving and the fear of nuclear war." In *The Journal of Conflict Resolution, 30*(3), 403–419, September 1986.

Taleb, Nassim Nicholas: *Antifragile: Things that Gain from Disorder*. New York: Random House, 2014.

Taleb, Nassim Nicholas: *The Black Swan*. New York: Random House, 2010.

Ueding, Gert (ed.): *Historisches Wörterbuch der Rhetorik* (12 volumes). Berlin/New York: Walter de Gruyter, 2015.

Vestrheim, Gjert: *Klassisk retorikk*. Oslo: Dreyers forlag, 2018.

Vickers, Brian: *In Defense of Rhetoric*. Cambridge: Clarendon Press, 1988.

World Commission on Environment and Development: *Our Common Future*. Oxford: Oxford University Press, 1987.

Yukl, Gary: *Leadership in Organizations* (8th edition) New Jersey: Pearson, 2013.

CHAPTER 4

Political Fear

Abstract This chapter explores the appeal to political fear. It is the fear that our society or culture may be at risk. This sort of fear reminds us that our shared rules, rituals, and regulations might be threatened. We analyse speeches of leaders like Jimmy Carter, Angela Merkel, Marine Le Pen, Horst Seehofer, and Comical Ali, and look at how dystopian stories may help us to craft an appeal to political fear. The chapter aims to help leaders to give an adequate assessment of the situation at hand to compose a credible appeal to fear and to use that appeal to help the audience prioritize between potentially conflicting fears.

Keywords Political fear · Hope · Polis · Migration · Climate crisis · Dystopian stories · The Hunger Games · Globalization · Glocal fear · Symmetric threat · Asymmetric threat · Kairos · Naming reality · Political adversary

HAND IN HAND WE STAND, ALL ACROSS THE LAND

On August 23, 1989, two million people in the Baltic countries, Estonia, Latvia, and Lithuania joined hands to form a human chain of more than 600 kms. In rural areas, where population was scarce, buses were brought in, so that the chain could be complete and send a clear message to the

B. Norheim and J. Haga, *The Three Fears Every Leader Has to Know*, https://doi.org/10.1007/978-3-031-08984-8_4

world: We want freedom! The Baltic Chain served as a peaceful statement to mark the fight for independence from the Soviet Union. People were holding hands, chanting, singing, and sometimes waving to the cameras, as the international press reported from the event. The video recordings of the human chain became a powerful banner for the Baltic fight for freedom and democracy. The demonstration was held on Black Ribbon Day, which was a day protesting the Molotov-Ribbentrop pact of 23 August 1939. The secret protocols of the pact divided Eastern Europe into spheres of influence and enabled the outbreak of the Second World War, as Nazi-German forces invaded Poland a week later. It also led to the Soviet occupation of the Baltic countries in 1940.[1] Similar human chains have been formed in many parts of the world, where masses of people link together as a sign of political solidarity. In 2020 approximately 43 million people gathered over 18.000 kms in Bihar, India, to support the government's efforts towards environment conservation and eradication of social evils.[2]

A human chain is a powerful way to address political fear. It forms an antidote to the most prominent threats at a particular time and place. Human chains are also an example of how fear and hope are closely connected. What makes a human chain hopeful is its capacity to serve as an antithesis to the most dominant political fear. By drawing on the feeling of fear and showcasing hopeful action, a human chain signals that change is possible. A new era is about to come. Human chains have also been used to provide hope for political change in the face of the climate crisis. Climate protesters around the world have gathered to form human chains to signal that another political order should be established.[3]

A human chain is an intentional speech act to propose the need for a new social and political order. It also appeals to fear. For those in power, the human fear evokes the fear that they may be overturned by the people. For the people holding hands, the chain reminds of the fear that the current window of opportunity, the possibility of a new political order, may pass unless they protest and act. For the Soviet authorities the Baltic chain appealed to the fear of a people's revolution, the fear that the communist rule would be overturned by the will of the people. That latter fear turned out to be justified. During the year 1991 all the three Baltic countries had reclaimed their independence.

POLITICAL FEAR AS A CRISIS OF CONFIDENCE

The appeal to political fear denotes that the place we inhabit as a community is threatened. Our *polis* may collapse. It is the fear that the political order is at risk. In his "crisis of confidence" speech in 1979, US President Jimmy Carter appealed to an imminent political fear. For Carter it was a national fear, namely a threat to the American way of life. The threat was "nearly invisible in ordinary ways," Carter maintained, but it was still a crisis that struck "at the very heart and soul and spirit of our national will." The fear Carter here expressed was the fear that an erosion of Americans' confidence in the future would destroy "the social and political fabric of America." The political fear Carter addressed had distinct nationalistic connotations. It concerned "the growing doubt about the meaning of our own lives and in the loss of a unity of purpose for our nation."[4]

Carter's appeal to fear was an appeal to political fear. It was the fear that "the social and political fabric of America" would erode or collapse. What Carter described, was not systemic corrosion, in the sense that the legal system was about to break down. Rather, Carter described how the American *polis* was at risk because the American dream was about to falter and faint. And this potential collapse would threaten the very idea of America, namely the idea of freedom and limitless opportunities. In his speech, Carter connected the ongoing energy crisis with the very existence of the American nation and her search for freedom and growth:

> Energy will be the immediate test of our ability to unite this nation, and it can also be the standard around which we rally. On the battlefield of energy, we can win for our nation a new confidence, and we can seize control again of our common destiny.

The vision that was the centrepiece of Carter's political exhortations was the dream of becoming self-supplied with energy. In his speech, Carter reminded the audience that exactly three years ago, in 1976, Carter accepted the nomination for President. The speech in July 1979 therefore served as a renewed opening speech for Carter, recharging the vision that he had set at the beginning of his presidency. In the "crisis of confidence"-speech, he presented a clear and ambitious goal for the energy policy of the United States in the future:

> Beginning this moment, this nation will never use more foreign oil than we did in 1977—never. From now on, every new addition to our demand for energy will be met from our own production and our own conservation. The generation-long growth in our dependence on foreign oil will be stopped dead in its tracks right now and then reversed as we move through the 1980s.

Carter also made it clear how his political priorities would be, claiming that "we will protect our environment. But when this nation critically needs a refinery or a pipeline, we will build it." For Carter the prime fear was the fear that the United States would be dependent on foreign energy supply. The fear produced a political programme, the goal of becoming self-supplied with energy. Carter framed his challenge as a crisis of confidence, which was simultaneously a sort of political fear. The American political fear was contained in the following future scenario: What if there would not be enough oil to grease the American economy and keep it running to ensure continued economic growth? How would the nation then secure welfare and prosperity and assure the American dream of freedom and unlimited opportunities for all?

We see in Carter's speech that an appeal to political fear often contains an implicit or explicit appeal to hope. In Carter's case, it was the hope that it is possible to secure a particular political order, revive a cultural legacy and make it thrive. In the case of the Baltic chain, the human chain envisioned the hope of a new social and political order, which was aimed at breaking the bonds of the Molotov-Ribbentrop pact.

Carter's appeal to political fear tried to urge the American people to act. Towards the end of his address to the nation the President used a grand style of speech to encourage Americans to place their confidence in the "rebirth of the American spirit":

> I have seen the strength of America in the inexhaustible resources of our people. In the days to come, let us renew that strength in the struggle for an energy-secure nation. (...) Let your voice be heard. Whenever you have a chance, say something good about our country. With God's help and for the sake of our nation, it is time for us to join hands in America. Let us commit ourselves together to a rebirth of the American spirit. Working together with our common faith we cannot fail.

Carter's closing of his speech is a typical example of how the appeal to political fear is often countered with a corresponding appeal to a political hope, a vision of a preferred future that the audience can commit themselves to.

MIGRATION AND THE APPEAL TO POLITICAL FEAR

On October 7, 2015, German Chancellor Angela Merkel addressed the European parliament on the emerging migration crisis. She shared the podium with French President François Hollande. They were the first heads of state and government to take the floor together since French President François Mitterrand and German Chancellor Helmut Kohl spoke to the European Parliament together in 1989. In her speech Merkel maintained that "the huge number of refugees is a test of historic proportions." She also described the crisis as a European and global challenge. Merkel appealed to the political fear of protectionism and nationalism as she admonished the audience:

> We must now resist the temptation to fall back into national government action. Right now, we need more Europe! Germany and France are ready. Only together will we in Europe succeed in reducing the global causes of flight and expulsion. We can protect our external borders successfully only if we do something to deal with the many crises in our neighbourhood.[5]

Later in the session, Merkel once again seized the word and addressed the European parliament underlining that without coming together, Europe cannot advance. Finally, the Chancellor stressed that Europe could boast many successes, such as the preparation of the climate conference: "A good climate conference is also a way of helping prevent refugee crises," Merkel argued. The political fear of the refugee crisis was expressed in the claim that the increased influx of migrants would threaten the political order and culture in Europe. Merkel's response to that fear was to appeal to European unity. She also highlighted how a well-founded and rational climate policy could prevent a future refugee crisis.

More than one million refugees made their way to Europe in 2015. They were travelling across the Mediterranean Sea or from Turkey through Southeast Europe. Almost 50% were Syrian refugees, making this migrant crisis another political challenge stemming from oil and energy conflicts. Many of the refugees were young, and it was estimated that approximately 4000 migrants lost their lives while crossing the sea to Europe in 2015, ten times more than in 2014.

Whereas the initial response to the crisis was welcoming and celebratory in most countries. The tone changed as the crisis escalated, and some government responses became more reluctant or even hostile. On June 17, 2015, Hungarian Prime Minister Viktor Orbàn announced the construction of a 175 km long and 4-meter-high fence on the Hungarian-Serbian border. The aim was to prevent illegal refugees from entering Hungary through what was now known as "the Balkan route." However, the response in Germany, the most attractive country for many migrants, was for a long while generally positive.

Merkel's approach to the refugee crisis was met with much criticism. Even within the meeting at the European Parliament such critique surfaced. Marine Le Pen, President of the National Rally in France (formerly the National Front) and Speaker for the Europe of Nations and Freedoms Group, took an ironic approach to Merkel's appeal to European unity. She also harshly criticized Hollande for being governed by Berlin:

> Thank you, Ms Merkel, for doing us the honour of coming here with Mr Vice-Chancellor of France Province. I cannot call you 'President', because you no more exercise your role than your predecessor did. The President of the Republic is the guarantor of the French Constitution. He must not submit to a policy decided in Berlin, Brussels or Washington, but defend our sovereignty. Yet this is not what you do. On the contrary, when, in a perfectly irresponsible gesture, Chancellor Merkel says that we must welcome thousands of migrants, you applaud with both hands. When a little later, she closes her frontiers, you're still applauding.

NAVIGATING CONFLICTING POLITICAL FEARS

When a leader is faced with a threat or a crisis, she has to decide which fears to prioritize. The case of the 2015 migration crisis is a typical example of how a leader often has to navigate between conflicting, and shifting, political fears in her appeal to the public. During the autumn months of 2015 public debate on migration in Europe changed: Political fear, like the fear of losing privileges or losing jobs, or even the fear of an increase in sexual assaults and terror attacks became more prominent. A leader of state who wants to make a well-founded and credible appear to fear needs to relate to shifting perceptions of reality. With the terror attacks in Paris (November 2015), Brussels (March 2016), and Nice (July 2016), and other terror attacks on Western European soil during the summer of 2016, the public and political opinion in Europe changed, and Merkel's initial appeal to a European culture of hospitality had to be framed in a different manner.

Overcoming fear is not simple, and for a speaker who wants to appear credible and trustworthy, she needs to acknowledge the strength of the present narrative of fear: Such a narrative may be both global and local at the same time: The effects of globalization, in this case, migration, seem to leave many people to fear the security of their social and cultural location. To fully understand the power and effect of a fear that is both global and local at the same time, the fear is perhaps best described as *glocal* fear. "Glocal" here refers to the presence of both universalizing and particularizing tendencies in the process of globalization.[6]

As we have already pointed out, the phenomenon of fear relates to how we conceive of the future. Fear has to do with the anticipation of evil or pain. In dealing with political fear, the speaker therefore needs to address the future. However, people are not necessarily as mesmerized by sweet talk about the future as one would think. Most people are intuitively sceptical to a salesman who promises a bright and promising future if you just buy his merchandise. Human beings learn from experience that inspirational talks about the future also implies an appeal to change and perhaps even an element of suffering. As human beings are driven by loss aversion, we tend to give priority to bad news. This implies that the human brain responds quickly to threats and anxieties, even to purely symbolic threats, as a sort of survival instinct. Loss aversion is a powerful conservative force, implying that we are more likely to favour minimal changes to the status quo.

To better understand the challenges of political fear that are glocal in nature and effect, let us consider how sociologist Ulrich Beck interprets the dynamics of fear in a globalized world. Back in 1986 Beck coined the term *risk society*, which describes a way of life that wrestles with the side effects of modernization. In further studies Beck used the term *world risk society*. The ultimate difference between the two ways of relating to the world, is that the first is terror-free, while the latter is security-driven. In our current "world risk society" fear seems to determine people's general attitude towards life, and security has displaced freedom and equality on the top of the scale of values.

In a security-driven society, people easily become obsessed with threats. Ulrich Beck has suggested a distinction between two different kinds of threats. The "old" kind of threat is *asymmetric* in that its effects usually follow the social-hierarchical order. In other words, the upper class may escape such threats by economic compensation or by moving away from the potential effects of a particular threat. In other words, if a place is affected by a flood, the affluent elite could find means to avoid the threat. The challenge of migration may be seen as such an asymmetric "threat." It is asymmetrical in the sense that the global elite may buy themselves out of the problems caused by migration by moving to a new neighbourhood. However, as the threat of migration to Europe was paired with terrorism, the logic of fear shifted. Beck has argued that terrorism is a democratic or *symmetric* threat. The essential difference between asymmetric threats and symmetric threats is that the latter can happen anywhere and anytime in a globalized world. As brutal as it may sound, terrorism perfectly fits the old slogan "think globally, act locally."[7]

Why is it so important for a leader to take time to better understand and name the reality of glocal fear? If a leader wants to persuade her audience, she needs to appear credible, in a particular context. Naming reality in a way that the listener recognizes as well-founded is key in gaining the trust of the audience. As we pointed out in our previous book, *The Four Speeches Every Leader has to Know*, the speaker has to *name reality* before *naming the cause*. If you name a cause, like "do not fear," it presupposes that this claim entails an adequate account of reality. In other words, if the call "do not fear," does *not* reflect a well-founded account of the current situation, the leader encouraging people not to fear could be in big trouble. If you want the audience to confide in you, it is not sufficient to simply name the cause. Naming reality first is key. In her address to the European Parliament in October 2015, Merkel described the migration crisis as a "test of historic proportions." This was an attempt to name reality: The German Chancellor portrayed the refugee crisis as a test of moral character. Having framed the crisis in that manner, she appealed to a particular political cause—to welcome large numbers of migrants to Europe.

CONFLICTING FEARS AND GLOBALIZATION

In Chapter 3 we looked at the Brundtland commission's report and its global optimism. Almost 40 years later it is worth revisiting the report from the perspective of political fear and the whole concept of globalization. Sociologist Zygmunt Bauman has mourned the effects of what he called "negative globalization." Bauman argued that a spectre of vulnerability hovers over the "negatively globalized" planet. The negative effect of globalization is that we are all in danger, and we are all dangers to each other. Bauman referenced a survey done in West Germany at the time when the terrorist organization the *Rote Arme Fraktion* scared the public. According to a study back in 1976 only 7% of German citizens considered personal safety to be a major political issue, whereas two years later a considerable majority of Germans found personal safety to be much more important than the combat against rising unemployment and increasing inflation.

As a result of this push towards personal safety, the global elite retreats into havens of security, where the SUV serves as the ultimate symbol of how a global consumer culture feeds on fear by offering safety and comfort to those who can afford it, Bauman has complained. Moreover, the global elite can always move and find themselves in a new place or another place, both Beck and Bauman have pointed out. If the local fears burden your comfort, and you have the resources, you move. The freedom to move freely is probably the most distinguishing freedom of all consumer society freedoms. Perhaps it is fair to say that those who speak favourably about risk-taking are not really taking risks. They have their back covered.[8]

With negative globalization the nation state is no longer an omnipotent master of its territory, Bauman argued. More than a decade after Bauman's pessimistic take on the fate of the nation state, it seems like the sociologist must stand corrected. The beginning of the 2020s marked a remarkable comeback for the nation state, not just with the corona pandemic and its national restrictions but Brexit and numerous events and political trends indicated a return of the power of the nation state. For many, the nation state offers a haven in a globalized world ridden by shifting fears. The revival of the nation state is a reminder of psychologist Sigmund Freud's argument that a particular characteristic of any group is that it usually has an extreme passion for authority. Simply put, a group wants to be governed by an unrestricted force, and in times of insecurity this passion for the exercise of authority and power becomes more imminent. The dynamics of glocal fear remind us that every speaker needs to reflect on the following dilemma: How do you calibrate the appeal to freedom and security as you address an emerging political crisis? A leader who wants to appeal to political fear in a well-founded manner needs to consider how to balance that appeal to freedom and security. This challenge becomes particularly important when threats are imminent, and the feeling of fear is leaking out of every crack in the fabric of society.

Addressing Your Adversary in Politics

Even in her home country Germany, Chancellor Angela Merkel was met with critique and disapproval as she encouraged the German people to welcome large numbers of migrants. Horst Seehofer, leader of the Christian Social Union, the Bavarian sister party of Merkel's Christian Democrats, condemned Merkel's decision to open Germany's borders to refugees fleeing the war zones in Syria. Seehofer issued an ultimatum to Merkel to change policy. He called on her to limit the number of migrants by All Saints Day, which at the time of Seehofer's ultimatum was less than a week ahead. He said that the situation in Bavaria was becoming unbearable and criticized Austria for its "open border" policy on refugees. "If I do not succeed, we need to consider what options we have," Seehofer argued. The Bavarian state leader's complaints about Merkel's migration policy were not new. He had earlier threatened to take the migrant crisis to the German constitutional court if the chancellor would fail to limit the number of migrants coming into Germany.[9]

Often in politics, political opponents will fight over which threats and fears to prioritize in a given situation. How should the speaker who wants to give a persuasive account of his view of reality and appeal to fear in an adequate manner relate to his potential political enemy? In classical political thought, the fear of war is the most fundamental fear. There are basically two kinds of war, war on external enemies and war against internal enemies, which means some sort of civil war. It may seem brutal to focus on enemies, but words like state, republic, society, and class are abstracts if you do not know who's your opponent. The most intense political contradiction is therefore the one between foe and friend.

There are obviously different ways to portray and challenge your opponent in public, even in more peaceful times. One way is to simply overlook and ignore the presence and argument of your adversary. You may also address your political foe in a more rational manner, displaying why you disagree with the core or gist of his argument. Another way to challenge your adversary is to address him on a more personal level, like claiming that he is poorly positioned to acknowledge or realize the impact of an emerging threat due to some personal deficiency. You can also challenge your political opponent more indirectly by referring to the misdeeds and weaknesses of a historical or fictional character that the audience understands alludes to or resembles your opponent.

How to relate to your opponent is a fundamental rhetorical dilemma in a conflict or crisis: Should you listen to your opponent, or should you confront and perhaps even demonize your rival? Or is there perhaps yet another way to approach the fears that your adversary is trying to install among the audience? In the New Testament, we can read the dialogue between Jesus and the Roman prefect, Pontius Pilate. Jesus' dilemma is a common challenge for many who have been faced with a corrupt or immoral adversary: What do you say to the evil powers when you are confronted with them? The response of Jesus is rather remarkable. He remains silent. He does not shake the hands of evil power and chooses a rhetorical strategy of negligence. In Chapter 3 we examined former US President Ronald Reagan's so-called "Evil empire"-speech. Here Reagan chose a different rhetorical approach, trying to portray his adversary as an example of how evil and original sin still rules the world.

Making a well-founded appeal to fear implies giving a convincing account of the situation at hand. The dilemma for the speaker is that a crisis offers ample opportunities to appeal to fear. There is always a whole host of potential threats and fears available, the question is which fear to prioritize when you speak. If you were the general secretary of NATO, facing the fear that the most prominent member of the alliance, United States threatens to withdraw a large portion of its resources: What fears would you appeal to in order to offer a persuasive argument to the American president, and how would you craft your message with the European public in mind? Or let us make a mental time travel back to Finland in the 1960s and 1970s. Imagine yourself in the shoes of former President Uhro Kekkonen. He had to navigate conflicting political fears, trying to calibrate Finland's rhetoric as it aimed to balance its position between the great neighbour in the East, the Soviet Union, and its wish to be part of the Nordic, and the West. The aim for Kekkonen was to maintain Finnish national independence, while not pissing off the aggressive superpower in the East. Let us then fast forward a few decades and consider another case that presents a dilemma of conflicting, political fears: The Nord Stream natural gas pipelines from Russia to continental Europe. For a political leader in Europe, it is sometimes hard to decide which fear to prioritize, the fear of insufficient energy supply or the fear of extended

Russian influence. On the 22nd of February 2022, German Chancellor Olaf Scholz announced that Germany will halt the Nord Stream 2 gas pipeline, which was built to bring more Russian gas to Germany. The Chancellor's announcement followed as a response after Russian President Vladimir Putin formally recognized two breakaway regions in Eastern Ukraine the night before. Two days later, on the 24th of February, Russia invaded Ukraine.[10]

WELCOME TO DYSTOPIA!

Yet another way to appeal to political fear is by describing a future dystopia and use this description to frame the challenges of the current political situation. Such an appeal to the political fears of a nearby dystopia can sometimes be effective. A politician may proclaim in parliament that if this legislation passes, our country is no longer a state based on justice and integrity, then we have submitted to anti-democratic forces. Similarly, movies depicting a future dystopia appeal to a vibrant and effective fear, namely the fear that our current social and political order is simply a prelude to what we can observe in the dystopian movie. The portrayed future dystopia therefore appeals to a contemporary, political fear: If we do not watch out, our political and cultural system may corrode into the dystopian chaos that the movie depicts.

The dystopian story of *The Hunger Games* is a series of three books which later gained worldwide attention and popularity through four box-office movies, with the fourth film being released in 2015. The Hunger Games offers a critical view on a future dystopian North America. The books were published at the end of George Bush Jr's era as American President (2001–2009). In the Hunger Games, most of the people in the fictional republic Panem live under extreme surveillance and control, divided into twelve districts. As a contrast, the rulers and people of the Capitol enjoy great prosperity.

The first book starts on the day of the *Reaping*, a ritual installed by the Capitol to force the people of Panem to commemorate the great disaster of the past, apparently a sort of civil war, which led to the establishment of the republic Panem. On the day of the Reaping each district has to carry out a lottery, selecting a female and a male tribute, aged 12–18 years. These tributes are then summoned to participate in the so-called Hunger Games. After the Reaping, the twenty-four tributes from the Districts are all sent off to rival in a bloody fight. The battle is cast in an artificial outdoor arena, where they are to fight until the last man or woman standing. The whole "show" is broadcasted live to all the twelve districts. The heroine of the Hunger Games, Katniss Everdeen, volunteers as a tribute from District 12, to replace her younger sister, Primrose who is 12 years old and becomes one of the selected tributes from the district. The other tribute is Peeta Melaark, the baker's son, who once saved Katniss from starvation.

The Hunger Games trilogy's attempt to describe a future totalitarian regime may be interpreted as an extreme appeal to political fear. Showcasing a future dystopian society, which aims to control the fate of its people by controlling their bodies, their food supply, and their minds, serves as a dystopian drama which indirectly offers a critique of contemporary political patterns, like warfare and regulations to control and limit the exercise of human freedom. It becomes clear that the narrative of the Hunger Games circles around a plot of fear management, where the rulers at Capitol aim to control the districts and contestants by regulating their food supply and energy supply. Dystopian stories, like the Hunger Games, may be influential, rhetorical tools for someone who wants to appeal to a particular political fear in a more poetic and even provocative manner.[11]

THE POLITICAL CRISIS AS A RHETORICAL OPPORTUNITY

If every situation is potent with fear, the appeal to fear is always present as a constructive and simultaneously destructive rhetorical opportunity. The appeal to fear makes explicit the common awareness that something has gone wrong or may go wrong. The appeal to fear announces the arrival of a crisis. A crisis may indicate the nearby arrival of a disaster, but it may also represent an opportunity to gain new insights and develop more novel theories for political problem-solving. Ironically, novel theories tend to emerge when we experience and then pronounce failures in the normal-solving activity.[12] In that sense a well-founded appeal to fear during a crisis may foster an awareness that helps us acknowledge failures and potentially lead to more nuanced and comprehensive theories. The appeal to fear is sometimes the wake-up call that makes the audience realize that we are facing a crisis. Subsequently, a crisis is often an appropriate prelude to the emergence of new theories for political problem-solving.

Crises are therefore not an absolute prerequisite to revolutions, they are only what we may call the usual prelude, supplying a sort of self-correcting mechanism which could ensure that the rigidity of how we usually do things will not remain forever unchallenged. A crisis loosens the rules of normal political puzzle-solving in ways that ultimately may permit a new political paradigm to emerge, potent with rhetorical opportunities. When a crisis strikes, it offers ample opportunities for the rhetoric of experts. Increased insecurity and fear for the future are fertile ground for political rhetoric where experts play a key role. In many countries during the corona pandemic, health experts became household names through their daily appearances in the media, people like Anders Tegnell in Sweden and Anthony Fauci in the United States. The fear of death or societal breakdown represented a rhetorical opportunity for the expert and the rhetoric of the expert. In times of great uncertainty, people tend to look for someone who can predict the future. Interestingly, some of the health experts in Norway even invited the people to act as experts. They asked the larger public: what should we do if we lose control of the pandemic?[13] This invitation to the people illustrates an imminent problem in liberal democracies when we are faced with a crisis. As most of us are no longer run by omnipotent kings, but by politicians who are up for re-election, news laws and regulations require some sort of voluntary consent from the public.

Faced with fear people might be more prone to accept autocratic measures and politics. In times of insecurity, we are likely to expect the role of an elite taking over control. Faced with fear, we may also feel more tempted to evoke old structures and hierarchies, like the bonds of family and the local community. A crisis challenges to prioritize between fears and hierarchies of fear. Typically, in a world of insecurity, where people faced the threat of sudden death perpetually, the rules of family and community seemed like the only guarantee of survival. The irony when a major crisis strikes is that the late modern modes of individualism seem like a luxury, almost like a dangerous indulgence.

What room is there then for the individual during a crisis? How should the speaker appeal to the individual and the individual's voluntary consent to a particular course of action when a crisis occurs? John Locke argued in his *Two Treatises of Government* (1661–1664) that political power should be understood as the power that every man has in his state of nature, and which he has given up into the hands of the society. In this lies a sort of tacit trust, that the governors of society will employ this power for the good and for the preservation of property. With Locke the importance of consent is emphasized.[14] This is an important reminder to the speaker who considers an appeal to fear. In a liberal democracy even the appeal to fear has to appeal to voluntary consent. The aim of the appeal has to be chosen freely and appear well-founded and rational. Even the politician who wants people to follow his suggested restrictions needs to appeal to the public to commit to new legislations voluntarily.

COMICAL ALI AND THE SEDUCTIVE POWER OF POSITIVE THINKING

Let us now shift our focus. We have looked at how a constructive appeal to fear implies making a well-founded account of the situation at hand, prioritizing between potentially conflicting fears. But what happens when the speaker fails to make a fitting account of the matter at hand, what does a less-founded appeal to fear look like? We have already examined British Prime Minister Neville Chamberlain's infamous exclamation at the verge of World War II, proclaiming "peace for our time." Chamberlain's salute has become the ultimate example of a less than adequate verbal account of the matter at hand.

The challenge for the speaker is to be able to evaluate what the situation demands and to interpret and address the felt fear of the audience. The problem when the speaker fails to make a fitting account of fear is evident. A vivid example of this sort of communication was brought to public attention during the invasion of Iraq in 2003. The Media and Foreign Affairs Minister under Iraqi President Saddam Hussein, Muhammed Saed Al Shahaf, rose to global fame, acting as a spokesman for the Arab Socialist Ba'ath party. Shahaf earned the nickname Comical Ali, or Baghdad Bob, because of his ability to provide positive and optimistic news at his daily press briefings during the invasion, even when the reality on the battlefield were much fiercer and did not quite correspond to Ali's depiction. At one point Ali announced that American soldiers were committing suicide "by the hundreds" outside the city of Baghdad. At yet another briefing he claimed that there were no American tanks in the Iraqi capital, while in fact they were only a few hundred metres away from the press conference. As Ali was speaking you could hear the combat sounds of American troops closing in on the venue. At the Minister's last public appearance on April 8, 2003, Ali declared that the Americans were going to "surrender or be burned in their tanks." When asked where he had obtained the information, he replied, "from authentic sources, many authentic sources." On June 25, 2003, the newspaper Daily Mirror reported that Ali had been captured by coalition forces at a roadblock in

Baghdad. The strategy of neglecting nearby fears and threats by broad-casting optimistic news coverage or even by offering light entertainment in times of crisis is a well-known strategy in many less-than-democratic countries when a crisis strikes, like for instance an uprising or even the outbreak of a civil war.[15]

DON'T PANIC, EVERYTHING WILL BE TAKEN CARE OF! LESSONS FROM CHERNOBYL

At the same time there is something quite tempting and soothing about this sort of oratory of positive thinking. After all, most of us seek some sort of comfort in the face of a crisis. When the two authors of this book were travelling together along the coastline of Tanzania in the mid-1990s, we ended up in a rather deserted place, at a small guesthouse. The host of the local guest house, a Catholic priest, responded to all our questions in a steadily comforting and repetitive manner: "Don't panic, everything will be taken care of." It was a tantalizing and attractive option to think that the priest was speaking the truth.

Here we have arrived at the dilemma of the audience, when faced with fear: Who should you trust? Should you put your faith in the enigmatic leader prophesying the arrival of a nearby catastrophe, or the pastoral comforter telling you that everything will be ok, or perhaps the more sober expert-politician using statistics, claiming that the numbers are up and are likely to stay that way? During the corona pandemic, this dilemma became evident in how leaders of state across the globe addressed the crisis in very different ways. Several leaders chose to emphasize the emergency of the pandemic using vivid imagery and metaphors to describe the crisis and introducing stark measures and restrictions as a response. Some were more akin to adopting the rhetorical approach of the Catholic priest described above "don't panic, everything will be taken care of," soft-pedalling the threat and the exigency of the crisis. Others again, adopted a more restricted approach, drawing on statistics and impersonating the mode of an expert when addressing the public.

Faced with the threats and fears of an emerging crisis, the public may find it hard to determine which appeal to fear that appears most persuasive and fitting. A decisive element here is the fact that governments and authorities could be tempted to deny obvious threats to avoid maximizing fears. In the aftermath of the Chernobyl nuclear accident in 1986, it became clear that Soviet authorities failed in their communication strategy. The public was not sufficiently informed of simple preventive actions in the few hours and days following the disaster, like the distribution of face masks and handing out potassium iodide tablets to block the absorption of radioiodine to prevent cancer. As it turns out, officials even failed to warn people to remain inside.[16] Obviously, downplaying the impact of an emerging threat, or withholding information from the public to prevent panic, is a strategy which could easily backfire as the harsh realities of a catastrophe becomes evident.

NAMING REALITY MEANS NAMING FEAR

In his "crisis of confidence"-speech in July 1979 US President Jimmy Carter was eager to give a convincing account of the emerging energy crisis. More than that, by appealing to certain political fears, like the fear of being reliant of foreign states, he proposed a future political vision of an energy-independent America. When German Chancellor Angela Merkel described the 2015 migrant crisis as a "historic test for Europe," she also appealed to a certain set of political fears. She encouraged fellow Germans and Europeans to consider the crisis as an opportunity to show the strength of Europe's political and cultural legacy.

The challenge in crisis communication is how to distinguish between a badly founded appeal to fear and a well-founded appeal to fear. The proof of the pudding is found in how a well-founded appeal to fear makes an account of reality that appears fitting, comprehensive and convincing. Therefore, the politician who wants to make a credible and persuasive appeal to fear must exercise the art of storytelling. She needs to persuade her listeners that her view on the state of things is the most telling. The speaker who most convincingly tells us which fears to prioritize, particularly if the feeling of crisis is imminent, is well-positioned to influence.

Let us consider a school headmaster facing budget cuts enforced by the city council. He needs to tell a convincing story of how to address the crisis. First, he needs to prove to the teachers that he can make an adequate assessment of the case. Then he needs to make a case to his superiors, pointing out why cutting budget is critical and should give rise to serious fears of decreased quality and perhaps even future security of the community.

Most politicians and leaders of companies and organizations would be well-acquainted with the need to prioritize. When you prioritize you make use of an implicit or explicit hierarchy of threats and fears as a rational basis for your argument. It can be crucial and crushing for a leader to appeal to the wrong kind of fear. A future-oriented politician will probably realize that tackling the climate crisis is the most prominent challenge or fear, at least in the long run. But if a matter of national security suddenly emerges, it is politically difficult not to prioritize what appears to be the most urgent fear, be it the threat of a sudden rise in unemployment that may cause unrest or even the danger of an unprecedented terror attack. The aim in addressing political fear is not to arrive at a sort of fear-free condition, but the purpose is to fear the right kind of things at the right time. Knowing which fear to prioritize, puts the speaker in the position to address the current situation in a persuasive manner. The challenge for any speaker is that you may throw away the audience's attention by calling them to fear a whole host of minor fears, and then losing the thread of the fears that really matters.

The speaker should also be attentive to the fact that it is the impact of *felt* fear, the perceived feeling of fear, that determines the hierarchy of fear for an audience. A particular fear may be statistically significant, but rhetorically less weighty. As an example, we may consider the fear of random violence by strangers. As a felt fear, this is a fear that seems to have increased rapidly. Statistics, however, show that such violence has decreased quite markedly in many contexts.[17] The rhetorical challenge at hand therefore always supersedes the simple account of facts. As a speaker, you need to relate meaningfully to the audience's perceived experience of fear if you want to make a well-founded appeal to fear. You cannot simply recount statistics or list bare facts. In other words, the speaker needs to address and portray a felt fear. This implies that there is an element of craftsmanship in all rhetoric, a creative space to construct persuasive metaphors, images, slogans, and symbols that speaks powerfully to the situation at hand. Classical, rhetorical theory emphasizes the importance of *kairos:* Finding the right things to say at the right time is the ultimate proof of not just a skilful orator, but a wise leader.[18] However, it is crucial that the argument you use is built to last, at least for a while. The appeal to fear, even political fear, should ideally relate to a fear that does not simply disappear the next day.

Notes

1. Misiunas, Romuald J. & Taagepera, Rein: *The Baltic States: Years of Dependence 1940–1990* (expanded edition). Berkeley and Los Angeles: University of California Press, 1993.
2. News report on human chains in Bihar, India: https://uk.news.yahoo.com/tens-millions-form-human-chain-120000515.html?guccounter= 1&guce_referrer=aHR0cHM6Ly93d3cuZ29vZ2xlLmNvbS8S8&guce_refe rrer_sig=AQAAAEMdXjjGJUQcw2vsQouHq0NdUs4Z-VousZCtivEO_ qEMUxRuHtxoYJJAZmIbak_4zV-UWVCBEGLbG49Q71sKI2McVz4 50M6jwk57dDsfoxk6ugMEjgHBEJqsBokojLikVxt-mchynJiVAopFVCn WLX_2RbTEhd7QuzyU22vDR1yR.
3. Climate protesters taking their cue from the human chain protest tradition: https://www.voanews.com/europe/thousands-form-human-chain-brussels-climate-change-demo.
4. President Jimmy Carter's speech to the American people on July 15, 1979: https://www.americanrhetoric.com/speeches/jimmycartercrisisofconfidence.htm.
5. Angela Merkel and Marine Le Pen's addresses to the European parliament October 7, 2015: https://www.europarl.europa.eu/news/en/press-room/20150929IPR94921/francois-hollande-and-angela-merkel-face-meps and speech transcript of Merkel's speech https://www.bundesregierung.de/breg-en/chancellor/statement-by-federal-chancellor-angela-merkel-to-the-european-parliament-806312. Cf also another speech from Merkel on the migrant crisis of 2015 being a historic test: https://www.dw.com/en/merkel-refugee-crisis-a-historic-test-of-europe/a-18784341.
6. For more on the concept of "glocal fear" and European migration crisis in 2015 and how it relates to globalization, see Norheim, Bård Eirik Hallesby: "Naming glocal fear in local youth ministry—And the migrating presence of Christ." In *European Journal of Theology*, 26(2), 162–172, 2017.
7. Beck, Ulrich: *World at Risk*. Cambridge: Polity Press, 2007.
8. Bauman, Zygmunt: *Liquid Fear*. Cambridge: Polity Press, 2007, 134–153.
9. Horst Seehofer, CSU-leader on the migration crisis in 2015: https://www.politico.eu/article/merkel-ultimatum-seehofer-refugees-given-deadline-open-border-policy-migration/.
10. See for instance, https://www.reuters.com/business/energy/germanys-scholz-halts-nord-stream-2-certification-2022-02-22/.
11. For more on The Hunger Games as a dystopian drama, see Norheim, Bård Eirik Hallesby (2016): "The Christian story of the body as the ritual plot for youth ministry." *Journal of Youth and Theology*, 15(1), 88–106, 2016.

12. Kuhn, Thomas S.: *The Structure of Scientific Revolutions* (3rd edition) Chicago: University of Chicago Press, 1996, 74–85.
13. https://www.nrk.no/norge/fhi-vil-ha-debatt-om-nye-koronatiltak-1.152 11853.
14. Locke, John: *Two Treatises of Government*. London: Everyman, 1997. First published in 1661–1664, 223, 224.
15. Speeches by Muhammed Saed Al Shahaf or Comical Ali alias Bagdad Bob: https://www.vg.no/nyheter/utenriks/i/0EjLmB/kom iske-ali-paa-tv-igjen and https://www.youtube.com/watch?v=vC5UTU AxgpE, and https://www.liveabout.com/baghdad-bob-quotes-4068522, and https://en.wikipedia.org/wiki/Muhammad_Saeed_al-Sahhaf.
16. Cf the following resources on the consequences of the Chernobyl accident in 1986: https://theieca.org/sites/default/files/conference-pre sentations/coce_2015_boulder/belyakov_alexander-84058471.pdf and https://www.nei.org/resources/fact-sheets/chernobyl-accident-and-its-consequences. Cf also the speeches by Mihail Gorbachew following the Chernobyl disaster: https://www.nytimes.com/1986/05/15/world/exc erpts-from-gorbachev-s-speech-on-chernobyl-accident.html and http://soviethistory.msu.edu/1985-2/meltdown-in-chernobyl/meltdown-in-che rnobyl-texts/first-address-on-chernobyl/.
17. Harrell, Erika: "Violent Victimization committed by strangers, 1993–2010." Published by U.S. Department of Justice, Office of Justice Programs, Bureau of Justice Statistics, December 2012: https://www.bjs.gov/content/pub/pdf/vvcs9310.pdf.
18. Consider for instance Philip Collins' emphasis on the importance of preparing content well in crafting a speech and giving attention to detail, Collins, Philip: *The Art of Speeches, and Presentations*. Chichester: Wiley, 2012, and how Max Atkinson describes how it is possible to paint pictures with words, Atkinson, Max: *Lend Me Your Ears*. Oxford: Oxford University Press, 2005, 215–243.

BIBLIOGRAPHY

Aristotle: *Rhetoric*. Mineola, New York: Dover, 2004.
Beck, Ulrich: *World at Risk*. Cambridge: Polity Press, 2007.
Bauman, Zygmunt: *Liquid Fear*. Cambridge: Polity Press, 2007.
Dryzek, J. S., & Lo, A. Y.: "Reason and rhetoric in climate communication." In *Environmental Politics*, 24(1), 1–16, 2015.
Farnsworth, Ward: *Farnsworth's Classical English Rhetoric*. Jaffrey: David R. Godine, 2011.
Fafner, Jørgen: *Tanke og tale. Den retoriske tradition i Vesteuropa*. Copenhagen: C. A. Reitzel, 1978.

Harrell, Erika: "Violent victimization committed by strangers, 1993–2010." Published by U.S. Department of Justice, Office of Justice Programs, Bureau of Justice Statistics, December 2012: https://www.bjs.gov/content/pub/pdf/vvcs9310.pdf.

Hulme, M.: *Why We Disagree about Climate Change: Understanding Controversy, Inaction and Opportunity.* Cambridge University Press, 2009.

Kuhn, Thomas S.: *The Structure of Scientific Revolutions* (3rd edition). Chicago: University of Chicago Press, 1996.

Latour, Bruno: *Down to Earth: Politics in the New Climatic Regime.* Cambridge: Polity Press, 2018.

Lausberg, Heinrich, et al. (ed.): *Handbook of Literary Rhetoric: A Foundation of Literary Study.* Leiden: Brill, 2002.

Locke, John: *Two Treatises of Government.* London: Everyman, 1997. First published in 1661–1664.

Misiunas, Romuald J. & Taagepera, Rein: *The Baltic States: Years of Dependence 1940–1990* (expanded edition). Berkeley and Los Angeles: University of California Press, 1993.

Norheim, Bård Eirik Hallesby: "Naming glocal fear in local youth ministry—And the migrating presence of Christ." In *European Journal of Theology*, 26(2), 162–172, 2017.

Poortinga, W., Spence, A., Whitmarsh, L., Capstick, S., & Pidgeon, N. F.: "Uncertain climate: An investigation into public scepticism about anthropogenic climate change." In *Global Environmental Change*, 21(3), 1015–1024, 2011.

Ross, D. G.: *Topic-Driven Environmental Rhetoric.* Routledge, 2017.

Stoknes, P. E.: *What We Think About When We Try Not To Think About Global Warming: Toward a New Psychology of Climate Action.* Chelsea Green Publishing, 2015.

Stump, Roger W.: *The Geography of Religion: Faith, Place, and Space.* New York: Rowman & Littlefield Publishers, 2008.

Taylor, Charles: *A Secular Age.* Cambridge, MA: The Belknap Press of Harvard University Press, 2007.

Ueding, Gert (ed.): *Historisches Wörterbuch der Rhetorik* (12 volumes). Berlin/New York: Walter de Gruyter, 2015.

Vestrheim, Gjert: *Klassisk retorikk.* Oslo: Dreyers forlag, 2018.

Vickers, Brian: *In Defense of Rhetoric.* Cambridge: Clarendon Press, 1988.

Wolchik, Sharon L. & Curry, Jane Leftwich: *Central and East European Politics: From Communism to Democracy.* Lanham, MD: Rowman & Littlefield, 2018.

CHAPTER 5

Private Fear

Abstract This chapter deals with the third type of fear, private fear. This is the fear that threatens the place we call home or our house. It may include the fear of losing your job, your family, your actual house, or even losing your sense of being true to yourself. This is the feeling that your authentic, autonomous, and perhaps even moral way of living, may be at risk. In this chapter, we analyse speeches from a wide variety of leaders, like Greta Thunberg, Al Pacino, Justin Trudeau, and Alexei Navalny. The reader will learn to know the power of appealing to shame and the importance of a deliberate exit strategy when appealing to fear.

Keywords Private fear · Shame · Authenticity · Autonomy · Oikos · Anxiety · Migrant crisis · Corona pandemic · Cancel culture · Public shaming · Putin · Strategy of exposure

KING MIDAS AND THE FEAR OF LOSING YOUR SELF

The ancient King Midas was the ruler of the country of Phrygia, in Asia Minor, the legend has it. The king was rich and fortunate in every way. He enjoyed life in abundance and great luxury and believed that ultimate happiness was provided by gold. He therefore found great pleasure in counting his golden coins, sometimes even covering his body with golden

B. Norheim and J. Haga, *The Three Fears Every Leader Has to Know*, https://doi.org/10.1007/978-3-031-08984-8_5

objects, as if he wanted to bath in them. One day King Midas was granted one wish by Dionysus, the god of wine and fertility, after the king had taken care of Dionysus' faithful companion, the satyr Silenus. The fortunate king contemplated for a while, and then said: "I wish that everything I touch becomes gold." Dionysus warned the king to consider the implications of what he asked for, but Midas remained steadfast in his desire. Dionysus could then do nothing else but to grant the king his wish.

The very next day, Midas rose from his bed with anticipation to check if the wish would become true. He soon realized that everything he touched instantly turned into gold—a chair, the carpet, the door, and his bathtub. Sitting down to have breakfast, the king tried to eat a grape, but the grape, too, turned into gold. The same happened as he tried to consume a slice of bread and drink a glass of water. He started to cry, and at that very moment his beloved daughter entered the room. When Midas hugged her, she turned into a golden statue. Full of despair, king Midas started to pray to Dionysus that he would take the wish away from him.[1]

Realizing the implications of his wish, King Midas had been struck by an almost paralyzing and benumbing fear. It felt like he was losing himself, as he could no longer relate to the world the way he used to. The king was still able to turn the whole world into gold, but he could not really interact with the world in any meaningful sense. More importantly, he was unable to express his true feelings to his loved ones, in particular his beloved daughter. King Midas had lost his sense of self. His wish of ultimate happiness had turned into a curse. He had been forced to question his whole way of living.

The fear of losing yourself is the fear that you are denied the opportunity to live an authentic life. It is the sneaky feeling that your current way of living implies a betrayal or denial of your true self. On the surface you may appear to possess freedom and exercise self-choice, but as you realize the implications of your actions, you are confronted with a surprising fear: What if I am really fooling myself? What if my current way of living is really betraying my true self? In the New Testament Jesus asks what good it will do for a man if he were to gain the whole world, but still forfeit his soul. The problem, Jesus points out, is what to give in exchange for your soul (Matthew 16:26). By the token of his wish, king Midas had corrupted his true self. Midas's sudden and surprising experience of losing his moral self and the warning extended by Jesus both point to what we here will call "private fear." It is the fear that your current course of action may be a deceit of your true self.

MY HOME IS MY CASTLE

The famous saying, "my home is my castle" alludes to the roots of what we understand by "private fear." It is the fear of losing your *oikos*, your house, and everything that belongs to your private sphere. An appeal to private fear is therefore an appeal to anything that pertains to your house in the broadest meaning—your economy, your family, your work, your status, and even your feeling of self. Appealing to private fear means appealing to the fear of losing your freedom. The appeal to private fear raises the listeners' awareness of what it means to be true to oneself.

In the book *The Concept of Anxiety* Danish Philosopher Søren Kierkegaard addressed the relationship between anxiety and fear. Kierkegaard explored how fear and freedom are related. Realizing that your options include anxiety, and as the number of options and opportunities increases for the individual, the possibility of fear and anxiety grows. The Danish Philosopher captured the existential side of private fear: As we become more and more creative in pursuing ways of authentic living, finding multiple modes of staying true to ourselves, we also become more vulnerable. To Kierkegaard fear or anxiety is complex and paradoxical. It is both attractive and repulsive at the same time, as we may both fear evil and fear good.[2]

In this book the term *private fear* refers to two things. First, it includes the concrete fear of losing the objects of your private sphere, like your house, your job, your income, your family, and even your life. Secondly, it includes the fear of losing oneself as a true person. It is the fear that your sense of self is threatened. It is the feeling that I may become someone I am ashamed of. By making choices that break with my true convictions, I violate my autonomy. Appealing to private fear therefore includes appealing to the fear of losing an external object, like a house or a job, and appealing to the fear of losing your true self. This dual side of private fear is well described in the mythical story of King Midas. An appeal to private fear could involve the introduction of new laws that limit the exercise of personal freedom. It could also involve the fear that your self-esteem and social status are at stake after a poor job performance. An appeal to private fear could even involve the fear of losing your job or your family. An example of private fear is the feeling of shame you may feel as you sense that your neighbour is looking at you in a surprisingly condescending way as you struggle to keep your kids in order.

How Dare You?

As a speaker you may appeal to private fear in different ways and on multiple levels. Appealing to the listener's fear of not being true to one's own self is an option, even when the climate crisis is on the agenda. The speaker may summon the individual listener to reflect on his or her own moral self, in the light of global warming. We have already looked at how the former President of the Maldives extended an appeal to apocalyptic fear to address the immeasurable challenges of the climate crisis. Similarly, we have considered different ways of appealing to political fear during the ongoing energy crisis, like Jimmy Carter's "crisis of confidence-speech." However, it is also possible to combine the appeal to apocalyptic fear or political fear with an address to the individual person's fear of losing her job or house, or even the fear of not being true to oneself.

When young Swedish climate activist Greta Thunberg addressed the UN climate summit on September 23, 2019, it was obvious that she was drawing on the apocalyptic fear that the world may be facing annihilation because of the climate crisis. However, if we examine her speech more carefully, we also notice a strong appeal to private fear, like the fear King Midas was overwhelmed with, and the fear that Jesus had in mind when he warned his listeners. Greta Thunberg proclaimed:

> People are suffering. People are dying. Entire ecosystems are collapsing. We are in the beginning of a mass extinction, and all you can talk about is money and fairy tales of eternal economic growth. How dare you!

Thunberg's catchy three-word warning "how dare you!" is an implicit appeal to private fear. Any individual or adult member of the audience is called to examine themselves in the light of Thunberg's warning: What if Thunberg is right, what if I really have lost myself in a fairy tale of "eternal, economic growth"? How dare I then face coming generations, let alone my own daughter or son, if I do not change my way of living? Will not a failure to act and work towards climate change be a betrayal of my true, moral self? How dare I?

In December 2018, a then 15-year-old Thunberg spoke to world leaders at the UN Climate Change COP24 Conference in Katowice, Poland. In her speech, Thunberg employed a similar appeal to private fear as she sought to confront the leaders in charge. She argued that civilization and the biosphere are being sacrificed so "that rich people in countries like mine can live in luxury." Thunberg exhorted her audience to consider how the sufferings of the many pay for the luxuries of the few as we look to the future with anticipation:

> The year 2078, I will celebrate my 75th birthday. If I have children, maybe they will spend that day with me. Maybe they will ask me about you. Maybe they will ask why you didn't do anything while there still was time to act.[3]

Thunberg's rhetoric here implied an appeal to the moral, individual self. Her appeal aimed to install private fear among her audience. The listeners were encouraged to consider what they plan to say to their grandchildren when they ask them about their fight for climate justice. Every individual person in the audience was challenged to consider the following question: Would I not betray myself if I do not rise to meet the challenge? The purpose of Thunberg's prophetic call was probably to inflict a sort of self-doubt, forcing the listeners to ask themselves: How dare I? Perhaps I need to fundamentally re-consider my wishes and action, just like king Midas, and seek a sort of repentance?

In January 2019, Greta Thunberg spoke to world leaders at a special address to the World Economic Forum in Davos. Here she was even more explicit in appealing to fear. She declared that she *wanted* her audience to feel fear:

> I want you to panic. I want you to feel the fear I feel every day. And then I want you to act. I want you to act as you would in a crisis. I want you to act as if our house is on fire. Because it is.

Thunberg explicitly appealed to the feeling of fear. She also claimed that the feeling of fear may be constructive as we face a climate crisis.[4]

Thunberg's appeal to private fear resembles the heed to sacrifice that a manager may employ in a dressing room speech, as he encourages each player to rise to the occasion and not betray his own ideals and that of the team. Al Pacino's famous speech from the 1999 movie *Any Given Sunday* does just that. Pacino's character is addressing a frustrated team of American footballers. He describes life as a "game of inches," and that you need to fight for each inch to stay true to yourself and to your dedication to the ideals of the team. The implicit fear in Pacino final appeal is that each player may betray himself and the player next to him if he does not stand up and accept the challenge of the moment, which includes sacrificing himself for a higher purpose:

> You got to look at the guy next to you. Look into his eyes! Now I think you're gonna see a guy who will go that inch with you. You're gonna see a guy who will sacrifice himself for this team because he knows, when it comes down to it, you're gonna do the same for him! That's a team, gentleman! And, either we heal, now, as a team, or we will die as individuals. That's football guys. That's all it is. Now, what are you gonna do?[5]

Appealing to private fear means speaking to the heart. If the appeal to apocalyptic fear implies an appeal to the stomach, where the aching fear that the end of the world may be near is situated, the appeal to political fear speaks to the mind, to our rational thinking. The appeal to private fear or the fear of losing yourself is an appeal to the listener's passion and to the heart of the audience. It is a call to stay true to yourself.

The Appeal to Shame

Simply put, the appeal to private fear aims to instil shame in the listener. Shame is a basic human feeling. It goes back to our childhood. Appealing to shame can be very effective if it is purposefully and carefully calibrated to the situation. Aristotle in *Rhetoric* defined shame as "pain or disturbance in regard to bad things, whether present, past, or future, which seems likely to involve us in discredit."[6] Shame can therefore be an effective tool in bringing up children. However, the implicit fear of shame can be evoked through a set of different, rhetorical strategies. One possibility is to appeal to hygiene. If you do not wash your hands, brush your teeth, or blow your nose, you are not clean enough to be part of a normal community.

Another way of instilling fear in children could be using humour and drama, for instance, by telling scary, but funny stories about a toilet monster or a tooth troll. Of course, you could also take the "short cut," and simply lay naked the plain fears of the traffic and make risky behaviour in the traffic something shameful. A more sophisticated way to appeal to the fear of shamefulness is to play on what is cool and not. You may, like the Norwegian soap producer Lano, produce a cool music video promoting the importance of washing your hands, which most kids would sing along to. During the Covid-19 pandemic many children channels, like Cartoon network, produced similar songs: "We gotta fight those germs. Don't touch your face. Wash your hands. Be clean. Be cool. Be safe. Be cool." By positively hyping the preferred behaviour and making good hygiene cool, you are implicitly shaming the alternative.[7]

An interesting thing to consider here is whether the child represents to us what Elemèr Hankiss labelled raw and potentially destructive nature. The rhetorical strategy of appealing to fear through shaming then serves the purpose of taming that nature. Rhetorically it is helpful to distinguish between shaming through moral condemnation and shaming through storytelling. Shaming through condemnation is easier to detect, but implicit shaming through storytelling might be more effective.

A crisis or a major change, like a war or a pandemic, may alter our perception of social norms and therefore even our understanding of shame. Such changes also influence the rhetorical framework, our perception of the situation. Every speaking leader needs to relate to such social norms as all communication makes us aware of explicit and implicit social norms in their attempt to persuade. Cancel culture and public shaming are phenomena that prove how effective shame may be as a tool to convince an audience of why something is more credible and plausible than something else. Public shaming is indeed a powerful tool. It can be used to control a group or even to motivate an organization. The point is that we tend to feel shame when we violate social norms that we hold to be fair and right. Shame is the feeling of being exposed and humiliated to the point where you are not able to look the other person in the eye. However, to really feel shame the person in question must be aware of having broken a norm that he or she finds to be desirable and binding. Rhetoric appealing to shame aims to make the audience aware of how they have broken with particular social norms.

The feeling of shame is situated on the border between the personal and the social. This is what makes shame so challenging, and simultaneously also what potentially makes the appeal to shame such a vibrant rhetorical tool. The appeal to shame may involve an appeal to disgust, which is effective because it shapes our intimacies. The appeal to private fear plays out differently when shaming becomes a common practice. The point is that in a culture of shaming the exercise of justice becomes democratized. In the era of social media, appealing to private fear with the help of shaming is just a click or keystroke away.[8]

Appealing to private fear by appealing to shame may be effective because shame regulates what we perceive to be legitimate and lawful. Obviously, that makes the legitimacy of the law into a fluid concept, as the perception of social shame constantly changes. Interestingly, heroes in dystopian books and films, like Katniss Everdeen in *The Hunger Games*, tend to find themselves to be above the law with a minor l, but not above the law with a capital L. In another dystopian movie, the *Matrix*, the protagonist Neo is admonished for not obeying by the rules:

> You have a problem with authority, Mr. Anderson. You believe you are special, that somehow the rules do not apply to you. Obviously, you are mistaken.[9]

No surprise therefore that the corona pandemic exercised our shaming reflexes. A rather absurd and ironic example of this sort of appeal to shaming took place in Norfolk, UK, during the first months of the pandemic in 2020. An NHS nurse posted on Facebook how she one morning had found a note left on her car, probably from a neighbour. The note read:

> I have been watching you travel every day (…) this is clearly unessential travel! You are part of the problem! … You have been reported![10]

The appeal to shame is particularly effective if we have to do with a contagious disease, like the coronavirus. We feel disgust for contagious diseases, that is a way of survival for human beings.

How to Inflict Shame on a Collective

How does the appeal to shame work on a more collective level? Appealing to national shame, or national pride for that matter, implicitly means appealing to a taste community. It is common with sport supporters: As a supporter you may feel disgust as you hear the chant of a rival team or see the jersey of the same team. Public shaming, of both individuals and groups, often leads to mortification. Unfortunately, therefore, the use of violence is often closely linked to shame. For some the use of violence may be seen as an attempt to restore confidence of self, as shame is a very self-conscious feeling.

The fundamental point here is that the feeling of shame threatens the self. In the rhetorical appeal to shame, the political purpose is to move from the space of self-perception to public perception. To meet the public eye, so to say. This sort of rhetoric of shaming was prominent even during the 2015 migration crisis in Europe. It turned out that that the appeal to shame was a particularly relevant feeling to appeal to because it presupposed a community, which at the same time was the community the migration crisis seemed to challenge. During the same crisis appeals to personal shame were used as rhetorical appeals to establish a collective national shame. Posts on social media would invite a very clear-cut *pro et contra*. Your stance on migration would determine whether you were a true Norwegian, German, or European.[11] The public rhetoric during the corona pandemic also rehearsed similar themes. In April 2020 we could read that Germany's response to the Covid-19 crisis put the UK to shame.[12] The corona crisis also created a new set of social rules. Suddenly, bodily gestures like hugging were found to be shameful. You were even supposed to feel shame if you moved beyond set borders.

No Christmas for You!

The 116th episode of the 90 s sitcom comedy series *Seinfeld* circles around a soup kitchen in Manhattan in New York and the eccentric chef who runs it. The episode is called *the Soup Nazi*. After standing in line just to get a taste of the famous Medium Turkey Chilli soup, comedian Jerry Seinfeld's friend George upsets the chef while ordering, as he complains about not getting any free bread with his soup. The Soup Nazi harshly proclaims, "no soup for you!" George's order is taken away immediately, and his money returned.[13]

A similar kind of threat was broadcasted by Canadian Prime Minister Justin Trudeau right before Christmas in 2020. He was less than pleased with his fellow Canadians' ability to follow the corona pandemic restrictions and threatened that there would be "no Christmas for you," unless you behave better. Following Canadian Thanksgiving celebrations in mid-October, the country had experienced a record peak of Covid-19 cases in mid-November. This caused Trudeau to warn that Christmas celebrations were in jeopardy, as the healthcare system would not be able to handle a repeat at Christmas. At a news conference, the Canadian PM appealed to his fellow countrymen in the following manner:

> Reducing your contacts, reducing your gatherings are going to be most important. And what we do in the coming days and weeks will determine what we get to do at Christmas.[14]

Trudeau's plea here implies an appeal to a private fear, namely the fear of missing out on a proper Christmas celebration, and the fear of betraying your neighbour's desire for a proper Christmas by being disobedient to the rules and restrictions. Appealing to private fear became a widespread rhetorical tool by government officials during the corona pandemic.

Let us now consider another appeal to private fear that appeared during the corona crisis, quite like Greta Thunberg's catchy appeal "how dare you?" The 2020 Red Cross report on climate challenges used the fear-induced responses to the corona crisis to argue for an urgent political response to climate change. The report presented an indirect appeal to shame. The implicit message was this: If we can tackle the corona crisis swiftly and boldly, we should be able to deal with the climate crisis in the same way. Probably it would even cost us less money, the report argued.[15]

Yet another appeal to fear during the pandemic was the appeal by governments and health officials that if people do not obey the restrictions and rules proposed, they might experience a similar mayhem or chaos like Italy, Sweden, the United States, Brazil, or India.[16] The list could go on, depending on where the crisis was most critical at the time of the appeal, and what sort of images would potentially be most effective in inducing fear. This appeal to fear operates on the border between private and political fear. It can be quite effective, as it both shames unpreferred behaviour and uses the appeal to private fear to rationalize why a certain response is the morally correct way to respond in the given situation.

The Emperor's New Clothes: Meet Wladimir the Underpants Poisoner

If we now return to the story of Midas, we later learn that Dionysus felt sorry for the misfortunate king and his plea for repentance and healing. Midas was therefore told to go to the river Pactolus and wash his hands. Rushing to do so, Midas was astonished to find that gold flew from his bare hands. When he went back home, the king found that everything he previously touched had returned to its original fashion. According to the myth, King Midas then hugged his daughter and announced that he would share his great fortune with his people. From that day on, Midas had become a better person, acting generously and living gratefully for the common good of his people. Following Midas's change of behaviour and repentant attitude, even his people were blessed with a prosperous life, and when the king died, the people all mourned their beloved king.

The turn in the story of King Midas teaches us an important thing about the appeal to private fear: Such an appeal often entails an expectation of repentance. The audience anticipates that the main character of a story will return to his true self as he faces the private fear of losing himself or betraying his ideals. Telling a story which includes an appeal to private fear is therefore like watching a romantic comedy: You expect a decisive moment where the main persons are summoned to return to their first love or authentic commitment. This focal point of no return often exposes the true nature of the situation or the true character of the protagonist and the antagonist.

Appealing to private fear may therefore be a powerful tool for someone who tries to appeal to a breach in character. The appeal to shame may instil a sense of insecurity in the recipient: What do people think when they see me like this? How dare I present myself to the world in this manner? Interestingly, the appeal to private fear may be an effective tool of communication for those who remain lower down the rank than their opponent. In other words, the appeal to private fear offers the little one an opportunity to get the upper hand versus the big one: The peasant may challenge the king; the child could reprimand the adult. The literary folktale *The Emperor's New Clothes*, is an interesting proof to that point. The tale was written by Danish author Hans Christian Andersen in 1837. It tells the story of a self-centred emperor who gets exposed before his subjects because of his vanity.

The emperor in the folktale was so exceedingly fond of new clothes that he spent most of his time and all his money on being well dressed. One day two swindlers arrive at the capital city of his kingdom. They pose as weavers and promise to offer the king cloths that are so magnificent and beautiful that they become invisible to anyone who is unfit for his office, or who is unusually stupid. The king falls for the deception. After a long and secretive production process, the two swindlers tell the king that the new suit is ready to be used. The two so-called weavers mime dressing up the king with his new suit. Soon the king sets off on a pompous procession before the whole city. The townspeople express their awe and admiration as they observe the secret canopy, shouting out "Oh, how fine are the Emperor's new clothes! Don't they fit him to perfection?".

No one wants to admit that they see nothing but the king's underwear. The procession proceeds with success until a little child suddenly cries out: "But he hasn't got anything on!" The father tries to correct the child, but soon a whisper spreads through the crowds: "He hasn't anything on. A child says he hasn't anything on." Finally, the whole city cries out: "But he hasn't got anything on!" The Emperor tries to remain calm, but he feels a slight shiver, as he suspects that his subjects might be right. He admonishes himself to walk on steadfastly, prouder than ever, while his servants and noblemen hold the train high, although there is no train at all.[17]

An attempt to tell a modern-day version of this literary folktale took place in a Russian courtroom in February 2021. Russian opposition leader, lawyer, and anti-corruption activist, Alexei Navalny, has taken on the role as Russian President Vladimir Putin's nemesis. In his first years as an opposition politician, he used the tactic of becoming a minority stakeholder in major oil companies and banks to show up and ask awkward questions about loopholes in state finances as an indirect critique of Putin's rule. At the court hearing in February 2021, he positioned himself almost like the child in the H.C. Andersen story, trying to expose the Russian emperor. The point of the hearing was to determine whether Navalny was to remain in prison for several years to come. Putin's long-time critic delivered a short speech where he maintained his innocence and critiqued Russia's political and legal system for corruption and repression, blaming it all on Putin:

> The explanation is one man's hatred and fear — one man hiding in a bunker. I mortally offended him by surviving. I survived thanks to good people, thanks to pilots and doctors. And then I committed an even more serious offense: I didn't run and hide. Then something truly terrifying happened: I participated in the investigation of my own poisoning, and we proved, in fact, that Putin, using Russia's Federal Security Service, was responsible for this attempted murder. And that's driving this thieving little man in his bunker out of his mind. He's simply going insane as a result.[18]

What Navalny is pointing at happened half a year earlier. In August 2020 the Russian opposition leader was hospitalized after being poisoned with a Novichok nerve agent. Due to his serious medical condition, he was evacuated to a hospital in Berlin. A month later he was discharged and then accused Putin of being responsible for his poisoning. The following investigation indicated that agents from the Federal Security Service in Russia (FSB) had been involved. In mid-January 2021 Navalny returned to Russia and was detained after accusations of violating parole conditions, following a 2014 conviction. He then released a documentary called *Putin's Palace*, accusing Putin of corruption. In the documentary he aimed to expose the Russian emperor by telling the story of how Vladimir Putin had become the real owner of an enormous and lavish palace by the Black Sea through massive corruption and fraud.[19]

Following Navalny's arrest in the beginning of 2021, and the release of the documentary, mass protests across the country took place. In the short court speech on February 2, Navalny, like the kid in folktale, proclaimed that emperor Putin is naked, only wearing his underpants. Navalny even proposed a new nickname for the President—Wladimir the Underpants Prisoner:

> There are no popularity ratings. No massive support. There's none of that. Because it turns out that dealing with a political opponent who has no access to television and no political party merely requires trying to kill him with a chemical weapon. (…) Murder is the only way he knows how to fight. He'll go down in history as nothing but a poisoner. We all remember Alexander the Liberator [Alexander II] and Yaroslav the Wise [Yaroslav I]. Well, now we'll have Vladimir the Underpants Poisoner.

Navalny was later convicted to spend over two and a half years in a corrective labour colony in Vladimir Oblast.

Calling your adversary to repent or threatening to expose the true, and malicious ethos of your foe may be an effective way to appeal to private fear. Navalny obviously played on fear. He even used the appeal to a private fear to advance a particular political purpose. However, Navalny's rhetorical strategy seems to break with the conventions of political debate. But the customary rules of political communication are challenged in the face of crisis: Calling a state of emergency, Navalny tried to establish a new prophetic room for communication, where truth may be told, and where what is now hidden, shall be revealed. Navalny took the man, not the ball, so to say. He was like the new kid who takes on the ruling school-yard bully by performing a sort of shaming from below, appealing to Putin's private fear. And for good reason: Navalny's documentary of

Putin's palace was seen by hundreds of millions online. The documentary was directed at Putin's private fear, so that the whole world would see him as Navalny sees him.

Like Greta Thunberg's prophetic appeal to shame, Navalny's rhetorical strategy was a strategy of exposure. The lies and deceit shall be exposed or revealed. What is now concealed in darkness, shall come to the fore, and every tyrant should fear the consequences. There's also another rhetorical element that contributed to making Navalny more persuasive to many. He enacted the character of the martyr by displaying an extreme willingness to pursue sacrifice. This sort of reckless martyrdom may increase the appeal to private fear, for Putin and for other authoritarian regimes. Navalny's rhetoric signalled that he would stop at nothing to uncover lies and deceptions, not just of Putin's political regime, but of Putin himself. He attacked the hidden face of Putin's persona. Navalny appealed to the audience that Putin's *oikos*, or Putin's palace to be exact, was a moral bankruptcy.

Navalny's attitude here reminds us of Church Father Tertullian's instructions to Christians who were thrown to the lions in the Third Century during the persecutions by the Roman emperors. According to Tertullian, the martyrs should just proclaim "Sum Christianus!"—"I am a Christian!" If asked anything else, they were just to repeat the sentence. Being a Christian was the only thing which counted. Remaining a Christian was more precious than staying alive. Navalny's sacrificial approach to politics was geared to have Putin, and the audience, consider the importance of private fear. Navalny wanted to underline that what's at stake is a question of character, not mere politics. For such a rhetorical purpose, the appeal to shame and private fear may be effective.

What then did Alexei Navalny fear? The fear of the opposition leader was that the Russian people would remain passive, obedient, and ignorant. In his speech this fear was more prominent than Navalny's fear for his own life. This is how Navalny conceptualized and modelled the *ethos* or character of a martyr. He proclaimed that he was willing to sacrifice his own life by appealing to private fear, to overturn the rule of a morally bankrupt emperor. Navalny's hope was that one day the whole people of Russia would join the little child—Navalny—in pointing at the emperor and crying out: "but he hasn't got anything on!".

Addressing Your Adversary with an Appeal to Private Fear

If you aim to challenge the rule of political leaders, you may therefore appeal to shame and private fear. The book *Why Salvini Deserves Trust, Respect and Admiration* by political analyst Alex Green, a pseudonym, was published in the autumn of 2020. At first glance it looked like a serious publication praising Italian right-wing politician Matteo Salvini. He was the former Deputy Prime Minister of Italy. As a leader of the Northern League, Salvini was considered one of the main leaders of the wave of populist and neo-nationalist leaders focussing on de-globalization and protectionist politics across Europe.

However, what seemed like an ode in the form of a book was in fact an intentional ridicule of the politician. Despite the professional and respectful front page the book consisted of 110 entirely blank pages. Only the first page offered a short text: "Despite years of research, we could not find anything to say on the subject, so please feel free to use this book for your notes." In appealing to the shameful and shallow, literally "empty," character of Salvini, the book publication tried to offer a rhetorical appeal to a breach in Salvini's personality, like Navalny's rhetorical attack on Putin's character.[20]

How may then a leader use this sort of appeal to private fear constructively? Put bluntly, when may it be advantageous to shame your opponent? Let us imagine that you are the CEO of a new donut company trying to challenge the long-time monopoly of the local provider of donuts, Just Donuts Ltd. What would happen if the new kid in town, Donuts' Heaven, would hint at the long-time CEO of Just Donuts' breach in character to achieve some sort of market advantage? After all, it is well-known to all members of the local community that the CEO, Justin G. McFaakauf, quickly loses his temper and shouts angrily at both employees and customers. The first billboard ad for Donuts' Heaven is not all that subtle:

Imagine there's just donuts, and no insults come by.
Imagine you're in heaven, it's easy if you try.

Although morally questionable, appealing to a breach in your opponent's character may be effective, particularly in a highly competitive or polarized environment. But appealing to private fear, or shaming, is also a risky enterprise, as it may backfire. Unless it is absolutely evident to the audience that you are "punching from below," like Navalny tried to do by attacking a mightier opponent, the appeal to private fear may appear undignified and discredit the speaker more than the opponent.

THE OBJECTS OF PRIVATE FEAR

We have now explored how an appeal to private fear challenges the moral conception of the self. The other end of private fear is the fear of losing the objects that secure your home, your *oikos*, like your income or your actual house. Let us therefore imagine the following fictional dilemma: Young and ambitious Brenda Thorberg has just been appointed new CEO of Safe Scooters. The company is a traditional manufacturer of scooters for older people, running on fossil fuel. The new Dutch owners have decided to rebuild the whole set of factory buildings, introduce new eco-friendly technology, and make scooters run on battery technology, instead of gas. Much of the production will then be fully automatized. As a result, many of the current workers will lose their jobs. But some new positions will open up, as well.

Brenda's dilemma as CEO is how to address this change, as she announces the plans to her employers for the first time. Should she focus on how the renewal of Safe Scooters is a way to address the apocalyptic fear that the climate crisis represents? Or should she address the more political fear that the transition at least implicitly speaks into: By keeping the Safe Scooters factory in the UK, the company is trying to maintain a line of production that does not move all its businesses to China. And as such, the change is a small contribution to keep competence and jobs in the UK. But the real dilemma for Brenda is how to address the private fear, which most probably will kick in once the workers realize that their jobs are on the line. As soon as they hear about the dramatic change, many of them will probably think about how to manage their mortgage, or how to ensure savings for their kids' education.

In the late hours, Brenda is trying to draft a speech. She falters forth and back on how to start, but finally decides to begin her address in the following manner:

> Have you ever thought of what you want to tell your great grandchildren when they ask you about the past? How was life back then, granny? What did you enjoy doing? What was important to you? Well, I am still young,

but I have actually given it some thought. It is sort of crazy, but I some-times get this vivid image before my eyes, that I actually sit with my future great granddaughter in the garden. She is ten years old, and as a proof to my vanity, I imagine that they have named her Brenda, after her great grandmother.

Brenda pauses to look at the attentive but puzzled looks of her employers. She literally feels how they are all silently asking, "where is she going with this?" Sweeping the audience for at least a hint of a smile, she continues:

> Suddenly young Brenda asks me about what my dreams for the future were, when I was young. And then I start telling her about the climate crisis and the challenges we had to tackle. About the green transition. I would look her in the eyes, and then I would tell her the story of Safe Scooters. With a sense of pride, I would tell her how the company became a beacon for change and hope in a time of crisis. Now I want to tell that story to you...the same story I hope to tell young Brenda, perhaps 50 years from now.

Brenda Thorberg's approach here is quite bold, perhaps overly optimistic, and surely risky. By implicitly addressing the apocalyptic fear of the climate crisis and framing the make-over of the company as a way to respond to the crisis, she runs the danger of underestimating the power of private fear. After all, for the workers who will get the message that they will be redundant, they will be less likely to consider their unemployment as a worthy sacrifice in the name of coping with climate change.

Private fear comes, as we have seen, in two modes. First, private fear entails an appeal to not lose yourself but to stay true to your moral self. This sort of private fear appeals to shame. It is the same kind of private fear Greta Thunberg appealed to in her speeches, but she combined the appeal with an appeal to a more apocalyptic fear as well. However, an appeal to private fear may also imply a call to fear a near future where your house is no longer a safe place to live. The fear of losing your welfare is a version of this sort of private fear. This fear implies the fear of losing a set of objects that secure your life and your home. These are the things that have to do with the *oikos*, the house. Simply put, this second version of private fear has to do with economics, which literally means the laws of the house, *oiko-nomos* in Greek. An appeal to private fear is therefore something other than appealing to political fear. An appeal to private fear entails an appeal to the fear that your house, your private sphere, your family, and your economy will fall apart.

In October 2017, the minister for oil and energy in Norway at the time, Terje Søviknes, spoke at an oil and gas conference hosted by the worker's union. The conference was held on the Norwegian West Coast, in the oil capital, Stavanger. Søviknes argued that "increased activity in the oil industry is good for our welfare system." He found that many people tended to be carried away in the discussion about climate when they claim that "we do not depend on oil and gas." This was a big misunderstanding, the minister insisted:

> No other industry can replace the profitability of the oil and gas industry. And it is not like the oil and gas industry tilts the work related to climate change. Quite the contrary, the industry can be a positive contributor to reach the targets set.[21]

A secretary of state, like a minister of oil and energy, may appeal to private fear by describing how running out of oil will affect the private sphere. Describing how a breakdown in the oil and gas industry may threaten the structure of the welfare state is an effective way to induce private fear. Another object to fear which belongs to the private sphere is the fear that you will not be able to move freely. Historically, the freedom of movement is a commodity that was provided by and greased by the access to oil, succinctly expressed in the history of the car and the automobile industry. But with the new technical development of electrical batteries, this is no longer necessarily the case.

THE NEED FOR AN EXIT STRATEGY

When a leader addresses fear, the leader should also reflect on a possible *exit strategy*. This is particularly important as we consider the appeal to private fear. Should the speaker communicate that the situation causing the fear will pass if the audience acts in accordance with the speaker's suggested course of action? Or should he unpack the more pedagogical role of fear, calling the crisis a test of the listeners' moral character? In either case the description of the potential effect of fear must appear both realistic and probable.

Since most of us are no longer run by kings, but by politicians who are up for re-election, laws and regulations need some sort of voluntary subscription from the public. Even the appeal to private fear rests on some sort of voluntary consent to the communicated message. A political dilemma in modern, liberal democracies is therefore how to address large-scale political challenges, like climate change, within an operational framework of freedom as self-choice, where exercising freedom in a particular way is perceived as an authentic expression of the self. To put it bluntly, practicing a maximized version of freedom as self-choice often seems to be an obstacle in achieving a necessary common good, like saving the planet.

The suggested political changes put forward by the climate change movement, like eating less or no meat, or restricting travel, require that the larger public subscribe to these changes freely. This happens either through elections or by changing people's behaviour and their expression of personal freedom—or both. In other words, these are changes that may imply voluntarily restricting the exercise of personal freedom, by abstaining from moving freely or cutting down on meat-eating.

How may this challenge be addressed rhetorically? One way could be to try to draw lessons from the political tackling of the corona pandemic. When the Covid-19 pandemic "hit" liberal democracies, this created a sense of urgency that provided "fertile ground" for governing state bodies in many countries to introduce more authoritarian measures, which in turn restricted personal freedom. Obviously, the corona crisis made the public abstain from many goods, however one major problem remained: Although many authorities appealed to the public to subscribe to these measures voluntarily, the fundamental logic was not one of voluntarism, but of introducing new laws and restrictions by establishing a state of emergency. The rhetorical tipping point for any speaker is to identify what it takes to make your audience commit voluntarily to the suggested course of action that your appeal to fear entails.

Notes

1. For a more detailed account of the King Midas-legend, see for instance: Kimmel, Eric A.: *King Midas and Other Greek Myths*. Simon Schuster Children, 2016.
2. Kierkegaard, Søren: *The Concept of Anxiety* (Transl. by Alastair Hannay). New York: Liveright Publishing Corporation, 2014.

3. Greta Thunberg's speech in Katowice in 2018, at the Climate Change COP24-conference: https://www.gbnews.ch/greta-thunbergs-speech-to-the-world/.

4. References to the 'Our house is on fire speech' by Greta Thunberg: https://www.theguardian.com/environment/2019/jan/25/our-house-is-on-fire-greta-thunberg16-urges-leaders-to-act-on-climate and https://www.youtube.com/watch?v=M7dVF9xylaw.

5. Al Pacino's speech in the film *Any Given Sunday* (1999), transcript: https://www.americanrhetoric.com/MovieSpeeches/specialengagements/moviespeechonanygivensunday.html.

6. Aristotle: *Rhetoric*. Mineola, New York: Dover, 2004, 72.

7. For the Lano commercial, see: https://www.youtube.com/watch?v=syn8qDNvd-s. For the Cartoon Network piece, see: https://www.youtube.com/watch?v=XwnERjQ9Ew4.

8. Cf for instance Nussbaum, Martha: *Hiding from Humanity: Disgust, Shame and the Law*. Princeton: Princeton University Press, 2004 and Ronson, Jon: *So, you've Been Publicly Shamed*. London, Macmillan, 2015.

9. Speech quote from the *Matrix*: https://www.quotes.net/mquote/60275.

10. https://www.theguardian.com/society/2020/apr/18/duty-or-score-settling-rights-and-wrongs-of-corona-shaming.

11. Cf for instance Kjeldsen, Jens E.: "The Rhetoric of Shame in the immigration debate" (Proceedings of the Ninth Conference for the Study of Argumentation) (2015): https://www.researchgate.net/publication/332574639_The_rhetoric_of_shame_in_the_immigration_debate.

12. https://www.theguardian.com/world/2020/apr/22/the-german-response-to-the-covid-19-crisis-puts-the-uk-to-shame.

13. For an excerpt of the Seinfeld episode *The Soup Nazi*, see: https://www.youtube.com/watch?v=1jSTiKHOFEI.

14. Justin Trudeau to Canadians on missing out on Christmas in November 2020: https://edition.cnn.com/2020/11/13/world/canada-covid-thanksgiving-surge-trnd/index.html.

15. Red Cross report on handling the climate crisis based on the corona pandemic response: https://redcross.eu/latest-news/world-disasters-report-2020-the-global-response-to-climate-change-is-failing-people-in-most-need.

16. New Zealand's prime minister Jacinda Ardern referring to the fear of becoming like Italy in a speech on March 23, 2020: https://www.newshub.co.nz/home/politics/2020/03/coronavirus-prime-minister-jacinda-ardern-s-full-covid-19-speech.html.

17. Hans Christian Andersen's *The Emperor's New Clothes* in English: https://andersen.sdu.dk/vaerk/hersholt/TheEmperorsNewClothes_e.html.

18. Alexei Navalny's speech in court on February 2, 2021: https://meduza.io/en/feature/2021/02/02/vladimir-the-poisoner.

19. Alexei Navalny's documentary video on Putin's Palace by the Black Sea resort Gelendzhik: https://www.youtube.com/watch?v=ua1UFU9Z3LY and https://www.bbc.com/news/world-europe-56007943 Cf also Alexei Navalny on critiquing Putin's reliance on oil money: https://www.bbc.com/news/world-europe-16057045.
20. Green, Alex: *Why Salvini Deserves Truth, Respect, and Admiration.* Independently Published, 2021.
21. Terje Søviknes, former Norwegian minister for oil and energy, speaking at the oil and gas conference in October 2017 (our translation from Norwegian): https://frifagbevegelse.no/forside/-folk-tar-skammelig-feil-om-olje-mener-terje-soviknes-6.158.496172.8bd4f15583.

BIBLIOGRAPHY

Aristotle: *Rhetoric*. Mineola, New York: Dover, 2004.
Farnsworth, Ward: *Farnsworth's Classical English Rhetoric.* Jaffrey: David R. Godine, 2011.
Fafner, Jørgen: *Tanke og tale. Den retoriske tradition i Vesteuropa.* Copenhagen: C. A. Reitzel, 1978.
Kennedy, E. H., Beckley, T. M., McFarlane, B. L., & Nadeau, S.: "Why we don't "walk the talk": Understanding the environmental values/behaviour gap in Canada." In *Human Ecology Review*, 151–160, 2009.
Kimmel, Eric A.: *King Midas and Other Greek Myths.* Simon Schuster Children, 2016.
Kierkegaard, Søren: *The Concept of Anxiety* (Transl. by Alastair Hannay). New York: Liveright Publishing Corporation, 2014.
Lausberg, Heinrich, et al. (ed.): *Handbook of Literary Rhetoric: A Foundation of Literary Study.* Leiden: Brill, 2002.
Nussbaum, Martha: *Hiding from Humanity: Disgust, Shame and the Law.* Princeton: Princeton University Press, 2004.
Ronson, Jon: *So, You've Been Publicly Shamed.* London, Macmillan, 2015.
Ross, D. G.: *Topic-Driven Environmental Rhetoric.* Routledge, 2017.
Stoknes, P. E.: *What We Think About When We Try Not To Think About Global Warming: Toward a New Psychology of Climate Action.* Chelsea Green Publishing, 2015.
Young, W., Hwang, K., McDonald, S., & Oates, C. J.: "Sustainable consumption: Green consumer behaviour when purchasing products." In *Sustainable Development*, 18(1), 20–31, 2010.
Ueding, Gert (ed.): *Historisches Wörterbuch der Rhetorik* (12 volumes). Berlin/New York: Walter de Gruyter, 2015.

CHAPTER 6

Dressing Up to Address Fear

Abstract This chapter examines how the speaker should dress up to address all three kinds of fear. We discuss how the leader should use and develop her rhetorical wardrobe to appeal to fear in an adequate and credible manner. This implies that we explore what kind of words, metaphors, gestures, and styles of speech the leader should make use of when trying to bring forth the message. We also explain how the speaker's rhetorical bandwidth may be expanded by practice. We here emphasize the importance of the character the speaker takes on and the wisely calibrated use of genre to appeal to fear in a well-founded and convincing manner. All in all, the reader will learn how to speak with a character and tone that matches the fear you face, use a fitting style of speech, and know how to use your own rhetorical wardrobe when appealing to fear.

Keywords Rhetorical wardrobe · Rhetorical bandwidth · Genre or Style of Speech · Docere · Delectare · Movere · Genus subtile · Genus grande · Genus medium · Character · Captatio benevolentiae · Authenticity

B. Norheim and J. Haga, *The Three Fears Every Leader Has to Know*, https://doi.org/10.1007/978-3-031-08984-8_6

DRESSING UP AS DR. DOOM

Leadership is directed to the future, and a leader needs to respond to the fears and threats that appear on the horizon. If a crisis is emerging, people usually expect the leader to reflect the urgency of the situation by taking vigorous action. The leader's ability to name the current reality in the manner of a poet, needs to be balanced by the rhetorical handicraft of a politician, someone who responds to an unfolding threat and the fear it causes by proposing a course of action and making decisions. There is, however, another option for the leader who wants to approach the future in an even more radical manner. The leader may act as a sort of prophet, trying to foresee the future and predicting doomsday before it occurs.

Nicknamed Dr. Doom for his gloomy predictions, economics professor Nouriel Roubini at New York University gained global fame for predicting the 2008 financial crisis before it happened. On September 7, 2006, Roubini addressed an audience of economists at the International Monetary Fund and proclaimed that a crisis was about to emerge. He warned that the United States would face an oil shock, a dramatic decline in consumer confidence, a crisis in the real estate market, and finally a deep recession. With surprising accuracy, he portrayed the coming events of the financial crisis, homeowners failing to attend their mortgages, mortgage-supported securities falling apart, and the whole global financial system close to collapsing as a result. He even predicted the collapse of hedge funds, investment banks, and other major financial institutions like Fannie Mae and Freddie Mac.[1]

The immediate response Roubini got was reserved and sceptical, and he was not able to create a sense of fear strong enough to enforce action and changes. What was the problem? Wasn't Roubini capable of portraying the magnitude of the threat in a sufficient manner? Roubini's problem was that he did not really respond to a felt fear at the time. The current perception of reality was rather optimistic, as both unemployment and inflation rates remained low. His perceived *ethos* or character did not help him in convincing his audience either, as he was known as a perpetual pessimist. One year later, as the signs of the emerging crisis was clear to everyone who wanted to see, Roubini returned to the International Monetary Fund and was now received as a prophet.

What sort of lesson could a leader learn from Dr. Doom when considering how to appeal to emerging threats and fears in a constructive and well-founded manner? There is an obvious problem here: Being a prophet is usually a lonesome enterprise, and for a leader, it is key to attract followers. It is essential for the speaking leader to make the audience commit to his vision of the future, even if it is bleak and pessimistic and fear-evoking. You need to tell people why a certain path to the future is worth following. The more contested your perception of the future is, the more important it is to describe and name the current reality in a persuasive manner. Because your description of the situation at hand forms the rationale for any perceived understanding of the future. The future is always perilous and open, and the audience knows that. You cannot simply proclaim an upcoming doomsday and think that people will believe you and listen to your suggested course of action. If the leader is able to portray the magnitude and imminence of an emerging threat in a persuasive manner, it is much easier to argue why a certain course of action is required.

THE IMPORTANCE OF CHARACTER

When you appeal to fear, you invite the audience into an unfolding drama. You tell a story about the emerging future. If you want the listeners to believe your story, it is essential to take on an authentic and credible character that fits the story you are telling. If you compare the emerging threat to a fire, it is critical to take on a character that belongs to a story of fires, like a fireman. If you compare the coming challenges for your company to those of a city facing a foreign army threatening to invade the city, it is crucial to choose which role to enact in such a drama of warfare. Do you want to be the steadfast mayor standing by your people, or the bold and experienced army general, commanding your troops from the secret strategy room?

What makes a character credible in a drama of unfolding threats and fears? It comes down to what sort of characters we trust. Many of us are drawn to more complex characters, with noticeable strengths and deficiencies, simply because we expect the characters in a drama to mirror life itself. Therefore, elements of suffering, pain, deficiencies, and desires contribute to a credible story and make the characters of the drama more authentic. When you take on leadership you take on a creative role and become a participant in an unfolding drama. The purpose of this drama, from a rhetorical perspective, is to move the audience in such a manner that they want to follow the drama and the story to its completion. But it is the credible and complex characters that drive the plot of the story, the meaning, and intention of the drama.

To appear as an authentic character in a captivating narrative the speaker must use both words and gestures fitting to the character you impersonate. The way you look at the audience, the way you move your hands and use your voice should be seen as an appropriate response to the situation at hand and the unfolding of the story you are telling. However, just as important is the speaker's displayed ability to listen and take note of the other characters in the drama. Remember, the drama is not just a one-man show, but a story of multiple characters. This is even the case when a leader is giving a monologue speech in front of a huge crowd. It is essential for the leader to adjust his tone of speech, his accentuations, his speed, and his gestures to the response of the audience. By listening to how the mood in the room may be changing the speaker is better fit to compose his appeal to fear in a constructive and well-founded manner. To move the hearts and minds of the audience you cannot simply stick to your script. As a speaker you must be prepared for the unexpected. After all, you are a character in an unfolding drama. One way to signal to your audience that you are listening and participating in the ongoing drama is by using pauses, perhaps even hesitate at times to reflect your intention to appear thoughtful and attentive. A speaker who pauses and takes account of the change in atmosphere is usually perceived as more credible and authentic and is more likely to receive sympathy, even when appealing to fear.

To Decide Is to Kill

The fundamental question when a crisis strikes is this: Who is able to deal with death and address the fear of death in a well-founded and persuasive manner? That person becomes a leader. Faced with death and the scent of fear, the leader also faces the fear of failing. When a crisis strikes, making the wrong call becomes even more critical. Many leaders hesitate to make any decision at all, fearing that they will fall short. But making no decision is usually worse than any decision, particularly when fear is imminent. If a leader fails to make any decision, it may be taken as a lack of respect for his or her followers. They expect their leaders to make a call.

When you make a choice, you get rid of your options. The Latin word *decidere* literally means to "cut-off." There is a dramatic element in handling fear by making choices. The presence of fear often makes you realize the need to make a choice between different options. Having chosen one option, you are most likely to be cut off from the others. For a leader it is key to make evident to her audience *why* the proposed way forward is either necessary, more attractive than other options, or more legitimate than other alternatives, or possibly all of the three.

It comes down to this: Who are you most likely to trust faced with fear? Someone who is able to *describe* the imminent fears in a convincing manner, someone who *decides* what we should do, or perhaps someone who is able to look at the whole situation from the outside and *decipher* and admonish others? Or perhaps someone who is able to master a combination of the three different appeals?

The Importance of Genre

We have looked at the importance of impersonating an authentic and credible character when appealing to fear. As a leader addressing fear you may both take on the character of the old wise guy, the elevated army general, or perhaps even the more sober down to earth expert. The use of character is closely connected to the purpose of the speech. According to classical, rhetorical theory, every speech may have a threefold purpose. The speech could aim to inform the audience, or *docere* in Latin. The speech could also seek to entertain the listeners, or *delectare* in Latin. Finally, the speech could try to move people, or *movere* in Latin, typically with an appeal to the feelings of the audience.

The point for the speaker is to balance these three purposes as he tries to address fear in a given situation. Finding the most fitting style of speech is crucial as you consider how to deliver your message. This has to do with how you communicate your *ethos*, or your character. The leader who faces a crisis, must reflect on which character to take on as he addresses fear: Should you take on the role of the teacher, trying to inform the audience, or should you rather try to entertain them, being more of a clown, potentially helping them to forget their fears?

In classical, rhetorical theory these three purposes of speech correspond to three different styles of speech, namely *genus subtile, genus grande,* or *genus medium*. The first style of speech is *genus subtile*, usually known as the plain style of speech. This is a style of speech that the listener usually doesn't pay any particular attention to. It aims at being simple and straight, precise, and tasteful. Although it is the style closest to our daily language, it should exceed being simply a version of everyday language:

Even when using this style, it is essential to be well-prepared, although the style does not crave attention for its own sake. The style generally avoids strange or unusual words and is reluctant to apply figurative speech. Employing this style, one should strive to use simple sentences. The style is typically well-fit for teaching, in other words the use of *logos*-arguments. For an audience, the style appears rather neutral and sober. The style is typically used when you want to present a case in a rational manner. The purpose of the style is to inform or teach. The strength of the style is found in its ability to be sharp and precise, *acumen* in Latin.

Greta Thunberg used elements of this style in her speeches on the climate crisis when she described the more technical details of climate change. Even Angela Merkel employed the *genus subtile* in her detailed argument on nuclear energy plants. The German Chancellor used the same style of speech during the early stages of the corona pandemic as well, as she was lecturing the German public on the impact of the so-called R-rate, the infection rate.[2] Saudi-Arabian Prince bin Salman's speech on carbon capture was an attempt at using the plain style.

The second style of speech is called *genus grande*, or the grand style. This level of style usually functions as an opposite to the previous style, the *genus subtile*. Typically, the style focuses on elevated themes, like love, peace, war, hope, fear, etc. The genre may border towards poetry, and therefore differentiates itself from an everyday genre of speech in its selection of words, composition of sentences, and use of figurative speech. The grand style often makes use of neologisms and archaic expressions. Metaphors and allegories are commonplace. However, the configuration of sentences should not be too complicated. The point is rather the more formalized use of parallelisms, like Cesar's well-known famous saying *veni, vidi, vici*—"I came, I saw, I won."

The extensive use of repetition is also a typical characteristic of the grand style. As a result of this, the grand style usually appears rhythmical, almost like poetry. Fundamentally, the main purpose of the *genus grande* is to evoke *pathos*, which implies triggering the feelings of an audience. The problem, however, is that feelings are usually short-lived. Therefore, the grand style functions best in combination with the other styles of speech. Applying the *genus grande* is usually most effective towards the end of a speech. In a powerful opening speech, like a political speech, the calibration of suspense, however, is key. If we look at Sir Winston Churchill's famous World War II speeches they start with a lengthy introduction on the matter at hand, using *genus subtile*. However, the elevated finale of the speech is composed and performed in *genus grande*. We have also seen in Chapter 4 of this book, how former US President Jimmy Carter in his "crisis of confidence"-speech made use of the same mix of styles, ending with a grand style of speech appealing to the American people to commit to the vision he proposed.

The main purpose of the grand style is to move the audience. As the grand style is typically most often adopted at the end of a speech, it is quite rare for a speaker to unfold the full potential of this style during the opening moments of a speech. The grandiose *ethos* associated with the style implies that the audience would expect the style to be fitting for a president or a salesman, perhaps even a prophet, someone like Martin Luther King Jr, or perhaps even Greta Thunberg.

The third style of speech is called the *genus medium* or the middle style of speech. As the name indicates, the style is a sort of middle of the road between the two other styles, the plain and the grand style. The middle style combines features from both styles. As a result of this, the style is sometimes labelled the rich style. The *genus medium* is typically a style used when the speaker wants to give a praise speech, where the speaker commends the beauty of the bride or the hospitality of the host. The mode of style is playful, even in its use of language. The main purpose is not to evoke passion, but to appear lively. A potential downside to the style is that it may be perceived as too talkative and without nerve, because of its rather loose structure.

Obviously, the style works best where not too much is at stake and where the aim is to entertain the listeners, like in an epideictic speech. Usually, the style is best employed at the beginning of a speech, where the *ethos* of the speaker is being shaped. Using the middle style well is a way for the speaker to demonstrate his speaking skills. The style is well-fit to create a bond between the speaker and the audience. The key purpose of the speech is to entertain. The strength of the middle style is found in its mildness, which shows that the style is geared towards winning the goodwill of the audience, in Latin *captatio benevolentiae*. Perhaps Alexei Navalny's ironic address to the Russian court in February 2021 may be seen as an example of this playful style of speech. Nicknaming his adversary as "Wladmir the Underpants Prisoner," he surely aimed to entertain his audiences.

Any typology has its limitations, and the great Roman teacher of rhetoric, Quintilian, argued that the three different levels of style is not something absolute, but rather refer to different accentuations. One could therefore imagine an unlimited number of styles. The point is to use a style which fits the matter at hand. In other words, the use of style, like the appeal to fear, has to be well-founded and proportional. Most people would expect a prosecutor defending someone facing death penalty to use a grander style than someone prosecuting between the parties of an inheritance dispute. The point for the skilled speaker is to have all three styles at hand during a speech. However, the composition of styles should be guided by the main rhetorical purpose, to speak to persuade. This means that contrary to what a modern reader may think, style is not something personal. It should not be an expression of the speaker's need to be true to himself or herself, rather the style follows the matter at hand, and the selection of style is directed by the aim to persuade.

The three styles represent a metaphorical bandwidth for the speaker to use. When a leader considers which rhetorical garments to pick out of her rhetorical wardrobe, she may take a more subtle approach, pursue a more epic register, or perhaps try to find the middle road. The idea is not to remain true to one style of speech all the time, but rather to consider thoughtfully which style to apply, given the situation at hand. Once a leader employs a particular style of speech, she also enacts a certain character. Or better, the audience associates the use of style with certain archetypical characters. If you draw on the plain style you may be perceived as a sort of *teacher*. The listeners may notice your fine and sober line of argument, and hopefully your ability to describe a theme or a matter with precision and clarity. The decisive thing for a teacher-type of speaker, employing the plain style of speech, is whether you know something that everybody knows or should know, and therefore making the obvious even more obvious. Or if you are trying to teach a new thing, like we saw with Angela Merkel during the beginning of the corona crisis.

If you use the grand style, you may be perceived as more presidential, almost like a *king*. Everyone then expects you to bring forth something out of the ordinary. The purpose of proposing such a character is to move the audience and to stir up their feelings, appealing to their deepest passion. Putting on the garments of your rhetorical wardrobe that makes you more presidential, also serves the purpose of seducing the audience. Not necessarily in the sense of fooling the listeners into something they do not want, but rather appealing them to direct their dedicated action to a particular vision of the future. The key here is the subtle and persuasive use of grandeur and the use of big words that appeal to both heart and minds, what speech writer Samuel Lancaster calls "winning minds." Here rhetoric and modern-day neuroscience finds common ground. Drawing on the grand style is usually fitting for the end of a visionary opening speech, possibly at the beginning of a crisis. During the corona crisis, we saw how many leaders of state used the grand style of speech with extensive use of metaphors to bring home the appeal to fear at press conferences, particularly during the first stages of the crisis.

Another way to employ the grand style is to enact the character and speech style of a *prophet*. Traditionally, a prophet is someone who challenges the ruling king and class at the castle. A prophet would often use persuasive metaphors and sometimes showcase grand speech acts or symbols all to offer an effective contrast to the lavishness and ignorance of the current leadership. Both Greta Thunberg's speeches and even the style of speech used by former President of the Maldives at the UN Climate Summit in 2009, Mohammed Nasheed, may be seen as an attempt to use the grand style to speak in the manner of a prophet.

The third option is to appear more poetic, like a party-host or a toast-master, setting the tune of a celebrative moment. The purpose for such a *poet* is to set an atmosphere of playfulness. You need to name reality in a festive manner, using the middle style of speech. The aim of this style of speech and the designated role of such a character is to mark that this moment is special, and we who are gathered here at this time form a community of destiny. Interestingly, Ronald Reagan's speech on the Evil Empire used elements of this poetic style. Reagan tried to describe what he considered a malicious opponent in a creative and sort of entertaining manner, at least to those siding with him.

Obviously, it is possible to appeal to all three fears within one speech. You may start by appealing to an apocalyptic fear and later convert it into a more political fear. Finally, you may end by appealing to private fear, like calling the audience not to betray their own virtues and ideals in this particular situation. As we have seen, one way to combine the appeal to different kinds of fear within one speech is by reflecting on the use of different styles of speech and the characters the leader may enact.

The means of persuasion the speaker uses when he appeals to fear by using different styles of speech also has a psychological dimension. By drawing on different styles, you apply different modes of influence as well. As a speaker you may appeal to the audience to submit to a particular authority. You may want to showcase yourself as the ultimate example of likeability. You may also appeal to a common and unified "we," for instance, by applying grand metaphors. You may even suggest a sort of "give and take"-situation, where the trade-offs are made clear for the listeners if they choose to follow your command or direction. You may also summon the audience to be true to themselves and a particular legacy in the face of an upcoming crisis. Once again, a delicate and wise mixture of the three styles may come to your rescue.

All in all, the three styles of speech and the characters you may enact when you employ them represent a register for the speaker to use. To give a well-founded appeal to fear, it is essential for the speaker to carefully consider and calibrate the style of speech and the corresponding character you try to enact. After all, a leader appealing to fear, who is not complacent with being taken for a simple demagogue, needs to construct a credible and persuasive whole. The message (*logos*), the portrayed character of the speaker (*ethos*), the style of speech, and use of genre should all support the appeal to fear (*pathos*). Only then, may the speech appears as a convincing and adequate account of reality which justifies the invitation to act based on the appeal to fear.

NOTES

1. For more on the story of Dr. Doom, cf for instance: https://www.nytimes.com/2008/08/17/magazine/17pessimist-t.html.
2. Angela Merkel's speech on the R-rate in April 2020: https://www.the guardian.com/world/2020/apr/16/angela-merkel-draws-on-science-background-in-covid-19-explainer-lockdown-exit and https://www.youtube.com/watch?v=22SQVZ4CeXA.

BIBLIOGRAPHY

Aristotle: *Rhetoric*. Mineola, New York: Dover, 2004.

Brunstad, Paul Otto: *Beslutningsvegring – et ledelsesproblem*. Oslo: Gyldendal Akademisk, 2017.

Cialdini, Robert: *Influence, New and Expanded: The Psychology of Persuasion*. New York: Harper Business, 2021.

Farnsworth, Ward: *Farnsworth's Classical English Rhetoric*. Jaffrey: David R. Godine, 2011.

Fafner, Jørgen: *Tanke og tale. Den retoriske tradition i Vesteuropa*. Copenhagen: C. A. Reitzel, 1978.

Hulme, M.: *Why We Disagree about Climate Change: Understanding Controversy, Inaction and Opportunity*. Cambridge: Cambridge University Press, 2009.

Lancaster, Simon: *Winning Minds: Secrets from the Language of Leadership.* London, Palgrave Macmillan, 2015.

Lausberg, Heinrich, et al. (ed.): *Handbook of Literary Rhetoric: A Foundation of Literary Study.* Leiden: Brill, 2002.

Moser, S. C., & Dilling, L.: *Creating a Climate for Change: Communicating Climate Change and Facilitating Social Change.* Cambridge University Press, 2007.

Norheim, Bård & Haga, Joar: *The Four Speeches. Every Leader Has to Know.* London: Palgrave Macmillan (Palgrave Pivot), 2020.

Quintillian: *The Orator's Education. Volume V: Books 11–12* (Ed. and Transl. by Donald A. Russell). Harvard: Harvard University Press, Loeb Classical Library.

Ueding, Gert (ed.): *Historisches Wörterbuch der Rhetorik* (12 volumes). Berlin/New York: Walter de Gruyter, 2015.

Vestrheim, Gjert (2018): *Klassisk retorikk.* Oslo: Dreyers forlag.

Vickers, Brian: *In Defense of Rhetoric.* Cambridge: Clarendon Press, 1988.

CHAPTER 7

The Virtue of Fear

Abstract The final chapter asks how the appeal to fear may serve as an appeal to act virtuously in the face of crisis. We argue that a threat—like a crisis of some sort—requires an adequate appeal to fear that helps the audience to respond to the emerging reality in a courageous manner. The aim is to show how to appeal to fear the right things at the right time and examine how an adequate response to fear may be courageous.

Keywords Virtue · Courage · Timing · Kairos · Suffering · Sacrifice

FEARING THE RIGHT THINGS AT THE RIGHT TIME

In the face of fear, it is essential to ask if the current danger appears to be real. It is critical for the speaker to assess if the object of fear is worthy of fear. If the answer is yes, the speaker could appeal to fear. The next thing to consider is how to calibrate the magnitude of the appeal. For the appeal to appear well-founded and persuasive, it is critical that the appeal to fear appears to be proportional. Only then will the appeal appear apt and timely.

Consider the following example: Jon Johnson, long-time CEO of the sea wind turbine company Oceans Apart Ltd receives information that a giant storm is on the way. The storm is of unprecedented magnitude

B. Norheim and J. Haga, *The Three Fears Every Leader Has to Know*, https://doi.org/10.1007/978-3-031-08984-8_7

and may damage and destroy the new windmill park. At an emergency company meeting Johnson cries out:

> Dear fellow citizens, this is the end of the world as we know it! Soon, our company and our dreams for the future will come to an end. So, I have three words for you: Run and hide ... Run and hide!

The first problem with CEO Johnson's appeal to fear here is that it appears out of proportions. It may be well-founded to fear that the company will come to an end because of the giant storm, but the appeal to "run and hide!" would probably leave the workers at Oceans Apart LTD quite baffled.

The second problem with CEO Johnson's appeal is that it goes against what most people expect from a leader in the face of a crisis. The leader may well appeal to fear in an adequate manner, but most people would expect the appeal to fear to be followed by a call to respond to the situation in a courageous way. CEO Johnson could have said something along the following lines, perhaps taking his cue from Al Pacino's speech in *Any Given Sunday*, which we reviewed in Chapter 5.

> As we face the storm coming, we must stay strong together. It will reveal our true character, not just as individuals, but even as a company. The storm is a call for us to be courageous. And therefore, we must face this storm with one eye on the storm and the other eye fixated on the guy next to you. Together, we will stand through the storm. Together we will be stronger than the storm.

A virtuous leader in the face of a crisis is someone who helps the audience to relate to the world by fearing the right things at the right time. The point for a leader, whether it is a leader of state or a leader of a major business, is to communicate a well-founded and adequate appeal to fear. Can this sort of leadership be considered virtuous? Are there any virtues to pursue in the face of fear?

A VIRTUOUS RESPONSE TO FEAR?

Simply running away in the face of danger was never considered courageous. Therefore, the appeal to fear and the call to act courageously during a crisis is closely connected. It stems from the idea that in a crisis the true character of a person or a company is revealed. In the face of fear, our virtues will show. When may it then be virtuous to appeal to fear? The simple answer is—when the threat is real. The point here is that an appeal to fear presupposes a response to that fear. And that response may be virtuous.

What sort of virtuous response may the speaker appeal to then in times of fear? The obvious answer is to summon the audience to be courageous in the face of fear. But what does it mean to be courageous? Courage is one of the four classic cardinal virtues in the Western tradition. To Aristotle courage was recognized as the virtue which represented the middle road between heedlessness and cowardice. The point for Aristotle is that practicing courage requires moderation. In other words, the risks that you may take on in the face of a crisis should be proportional to the ends you seek to fulfil. Courage, then, is a virtue when someone chooses to do good, even when the going gets tough, and there's a cost to your deeds and action. Usually, we tend to respect the courage which is expressed when people seem to take risks without selfish motivation. Simply put, courage is the expression of moral strength in the face of danger. More narrowly defined, courage is defined as the capacity to face death in feud or war. In a broader sense, courage is often understood as fortitude. Traditionally, courage was necessary to defend oneself and family from external threats. However, courage, much like loyalty, is a rather "grey" virtue, as it can be used to service both good and bad purposes. Many therefore claim courage is some sort of psychological mystery. Both moral philosophers and soldiers are interested in theorizing courage.[1]

It is also important to pay attention to another element here. Courage appears most virtuous when it is paired with knowledge and practical wisdom, what the Greeks used to call *phronesis*. An overall point for Aristotle is that a true virtue is worthy of cultivation. This means it is worth exercising and reflecting on to increase the influence of that virtue. Courage is a virtue that very few would question. It is in fact the first virtue Aristotle speaks about in detail in his treatment of virtues. Like with all virtues for Aristotle, even the virtue of courage points to a mean, a midpoint of moderation between extremes. According to Aristotle, both extremes should be avoided as they are expressions of either excess or a deficit. The excessive side of courage is to act in an overly bold manner. The deficient version of courage is to be paralyzed with fear.

What should we fear then? Aristotle argues that we should obviously fear all bad things, but if someone simply fears things that are fearful, this is not sufficient to call the person courageous. In other words, it is not the lack of fear, that makes someone courageous. It is the right calibration of fear, and the adequate response to fear that is courageous. As an example, Aristotle finds that it is right for a virtuous man to fear the loss of a good reputation. It would be quite absurd to propose that such a man is not courageous because he fears the loss of his reputation. It therefore comes down to the appropriateness of courage. It depends on the wise discernment of the situation and circumstances and what may be the most courageous response. In the Nicomachean Ethics Aristotle defines a courageous person in the following manner:

> The courageous man withstands and fears those things which it is necessary (to fear and withstand) and on account of the right of the right reason, and how and when it is necessary (to fear or withstand) them, and likewise in the case of being bold. (Nicomachean Ethics, 1116b17–19)

What should we make of this, as we consider a virtuous response to fear? For a soldier it may be an expression of hubris and rashness to simply race ahead of his troop. Similarly, one may consider whether certain expressions of climate change activism, where the activist goes completely solo and runs ahead of everything and everyone, is an expression of the same. Exercising courage in this manner may be seen as an expression of self-deception and hubris, not real courage. Courage, rather, shows itself in concerted and calibrated action, Aristotle argues. It is not the work of one man or woman alone. At the same time a possible critique of the Aristotelian understanding of courage as a means, is that it does not leave much communicative room for the prophet, who cries out alone in the wilderness: How dare you?

For the prophet there is often another virtue at play, namely justice. In her speech to the UN Climate Summit in 2019, Greta Thunberg appealed to justice as a virtue. The prophet's call to the audience therefore always entails a challenge to reflect on the following question: what is the just *and* courageous response to the crisis at hand?

How should a speaker then appeal to courage? Over and again, it depends on the situation at hand. Simply exhorting the audience to be courageous is less likely to succeed. The challenge for the speaker is to depict why change is necessary, given the circumstances. And subsequently why a certain courageous response, that may even entail an element of suffering, could lead to change and some sort of success or victory in the future. After all, who would like to sacrifice themselves for a lost cause?

An example of how the speaker may summon the audience to be courageous, while promising success, is found in the final section of his former US President Jimmy Carter "crisis of confidence"-speech. Facing the energy crisis, Carter exhorted the American people to be courageous. He even underlined that the situation required a sort of dedication and suffering, that "there is simply no way to avoid sacrifice." At the same time, Carter did not simply call the American people to be courageous and dedicate themselves to the cause to restore American confidence. He also proclaimed that he believed in future victory: "I firmly believe that we have the national will to win this war." The President also named the reality that provided the grounds for his hope for success:

> I have seen the strength of America in the inexhaustible resources of our people. In the days to come, let us renew that strength in the struggle for an energy-secure nation.

Finally, Carter combined the appeal to courage with the appeal to act together for future success: "Working together with our common faith we cannot fail."[2]

35 years later, American actor Leonardo di Caprio gave a short, but intense address to the UN climate summit in September 2014. In his speech he urged world leaders to act in response to the climate crisis. Di Caprio challenged the world leaders to show courage. At the end of his speech, he first appeared to *kairos*, arguing that "this is the most urgent of times, and the most urgent of messages." He then used an *ethos*-argument to amplify his message, which served as sort of an appeal to private fear, a sort of pretext

> Honoured delegates, leaders of the world, I pretend for a living. But you do not. The people made their voices heard on Sunday around the world and the momentum will not stop. And now it's YOUR turn, the time to answer the greatest challenge of our existence on this planet ... is now. I beg you to face it with courage. And honesty. Thank you.[3]

A virtuous response to fear is therefore not a question of appealing to mere recklessness. It comes down to exercising the discipline of acting wisely, based on a set of esteemed virtues, rather than on impulse.

Courage is the typical virtuous response to fear, and courage often manifests itself as valour and bravery. It could also be demonstrated through perseverance and endurance as an expression of integrity and honesty, often called moral courage. A courageous response could even be to "keep calm and carry on!" Faced with a crisis, it is sometimes more courageous to wait, and remain calm, not responding to the challenge by giving a passionate reply or perhaps even violent retaliation. The Baltic chain serves as an excellent example of how it may be courageous, and rhetorically effective, to keep calm together.

The appeal to virtue in the face of fear is an appeal to display character. It is the appeal to the *ethos* of the speaker and of the audience. It reminds the leader and her listeners not to fear anything but giving up on their ideals, which would imply betraying their own sacrifice. You hear elements of such appeals to virtue in pledges given by certain professions, like nurses, doctors, and priests, among others. Napoleon Bonaparte once spoke on how fear, virtue, and ethos are connected in his *Farewell to the Old Guard*:

> The people to fear are not those who disagree with you, but those who disagree with you and are too cowardly to let you know.[4]

Perhaps Napoleon's call may serve as a reminder of what it takes to keep an open and deliberative democratic public virtuous, namely by developing a culture of fair, well-founded, and adequate exchange of criticism and opinions.

Napoleon's appeal is also a reminder of how an orator relates to death in many ways and represents the ultimate test of a speaker's virtue. According to ancient, classical oratory death reveals the true nature of a person. Fundamentally death is something beautiful if it is a hero's death, but what makes a death heroic? A typical example is to die for one's country. Here we see that the proof of the pudding when it comes to virtue is not really the individual as such, it is the common good of the community. The only standard of true virtue, or *areté* in Greek, is therefore the common good of the city or community, the *polis*. Whatever strengthens or helps the community is good, whatever injures or jeopardizes it is bad. A good leader, or wise politician, is someone who addresses common concerns in a convincing and well-founded manner and suggests a persuasive vision for the future entailing an adequate course of action faced with a crisis.

In ancient Greece the politician is therefore simply called *rhétor*, or orator. Eloquence is the proof of true virtue. To fight for the common good is to articulate the common good. Therefore, even the education of leaders takes rhetoric or eloquence as its point of departure in its attempt to educate man for political leadership. Therefore, the aim of the educational movement led by the Sophists was never to educate the people as such but to educate the leaders of the people.

The Appeal to Fear as Reality Check

In this book we have looked at how a leader may appeal to fear in adequate ways and how the appeal to fear may serve a constructive purpose in a crisis, particularly in the face of the climate crisis. We have promoted the art of appealing to fear the right things at the right time, and for the right reasons.

The typology of the three fears we have explored in this book is connected to different aspects of the listeners' world. The first fear, *apocalyptic fear*, concerns the fear that nature itself is about to collapse. The second fear, *political fear*, is the fear that our political system and legacy are at risk. The third fear, *private fear*, is the fear that your family, your job, and even your sense of self are in danger. All three fears refer to a particular place. Throughout this book we have argued that an adequate and well-founded appeal to fear needs to make an account of reality, by naming the way things are at a particular place and at a particular time in a manner that persuades the audience. By making an account of a place and a time, the appeal to fear may be considered rational, in a certain sense: Simply put, a threat requires a well-founded appeal to fear.

Notes

1. Miller, William Ian: *The Mystery of Courage*. Cambridge, MA: Harvard University Press, 2002, 5, 8, 27, 29.
2. President Jimmy Carter's speech to the American people on July 15, 1979: https://www.americanrhetoric.com/speeches/jimmycartercrisisofco nfidence.htm.
3. Leonardo di Caprio's speech on September 23, 2014: https://www.thegua rdian.com/environment/2014/sep/23/leonarodo-dicaprio-un-climate- change-speech-new-york and https://www.youtube.com/watch?v=ka6_ 3TJcCkA.
4. Speech transcript from Napoleon Bonaparte's *Farewell to the Old Guard*: https://www.historyplace.com/speeches/napoleon.htm.

Bibliography

Aristotle: *The Nicomachean Ethics* (Transl. by J. A. K. Thomson). London: Penguin books, 2004.

Aristotle: *Rhetoric*. Mineola, New York: Dover, 2004.

Farnsworth, Ward: *Farnsworth's Classical English Rhetoric*. Jaffrey: David R. Godine, 2011.

Fafner, Jørgen: *Tanke og tale. Den retoriske tradition i Vesteuropa*. Copenhagen: C. A. Reitzel, 1978.

Humes, James C: *The Sir Winston Method. Five Secrets of Speaking the Language of Leadership*. New York: William Morrow & Company, 1991.

Jaeger, Werner: *Paideia: The Ideals of Greek Culture: Vol I Archaic Greece the Mind of Athens*. Oxford: Oxford University Press, 1967.

Lausberg, Heinrich, et al. (ed.): *Handbook of Literary Rhetoric: A Foundation of Literary Study*. Leiden: Brill, 2002.

Miller, William Ian: *The Mystery of Courage*. Cambridge, MA: Harvard University Press, 2002.

Moser, S. C., & Dilling, L.: *Creating a Climate for Change: Communicating Climate Change and Facilitating Social Change*. Cambridge University Press, 2007.

Norheim, Bård and Haga, Joar: *The Four Speeches. Every Leader Has to Know*. London: Palgrave Macmillan (Palgrave Pivot), 2020.

Quintillian: *The Orator's Education. Volume V: Books 11–12* (Ed. and Transl. by Donald A. Russell). Harvard: Harvard University Press, Loeb Classical Library.

Ueding, Gert (ed.): *Historisches Wörterbuch der Rhetorik* (12 volumes). Berlin/New York: Walter de Gruyter, 2015.

Vestrheim, Gjert: *Klassisk retorikk*. Oslo: Dreyers forlag, 2018.

Vickers, Brian: *In Defense of Rhetoric*. Cambridge: Clarendon Press, 1988.

Yukl, Gary: *Leadership in Organizations* (8th edition). Hoboken, NJ: Pearson, 2013.

Ten Commandments for a Crisis

For Leaders Who Want to Appeal to Fear in an Adequate Way

1. Fear the right things
2. Give an adequate assessment of the situation
3. Prioritize between conflicting fears
4. Balance *apocalyptic*, *political*, and *private* fear
5. Understand the fears of your audience
6. Tell why it is urgent
7. Present people with choices
8. Know your opponent
9. Use a character that fits the fear you face
10. Give courage a face

And always remember that a threat requires an appeal to fear.

BIBLIOGRAPHY

Andrew, Christopher & Gordievsky, Oleg: *Comrade Kryuchkov's Instructions: Top Secret Files on KGB Foreign Operations, 1975–1985*. Stanford, CA: Stanford University Press, 1993.

Arendt, Hannah: *The Human Condition*. Chicago: The University of Chicago Press, 1998.

Aristotle: *Rhetoric*. Mineola, New York: Dover, 2004.

Aristotle: *The Nicomachean Ethics* (Transl. by J. A. K. Thomson). London, Penguin Books, 2004.

Atkinson, Max: *Lend Me Your Ears*. Oxford: Oxford University Press, 2005.

Bauman, Zygmunt: *Liquid Fear*. Cambridge: Polity Press, 2007.

Beck, Ulrich: *World at Risk*. Cambridge: Polity Press, 2007.

Blair, John M.: *The Control of Oil*. New York: Pantheon Books, 1976.

Brunstad, Paul Otto: *Beslutningsvegring—et ledelsesproblem*. Oslo: Gyldendal Akademisk, 2017.

Cialdini, Robert: *Influence, New and Expanded: The Psychology of Persuasion*. New York: Harper Business, 2021.

Cantrill, J. G., & Oravec, C.: *The Symbolic Earth: Discourse and Our Creation of the Environment*. University Press of Kentucky, 1996.

Charteris-Black, Jonathan: *Politicians and Rhetoric: The Persuasive Power of Metaphor*. London: Palgrave Macmillan, 2011.

Collins, Philip: *The Art of Speeches, and Presentations*. Chichester: Wiley, 2012.

Darwin, Charles: *The Origin of Species by Means of Natural Selection*. London: Penguin books, 1985. First published by John Murray in 1859.

Dryzek, J. S., & Lo, A. Y.: Reason and rhetoric in climate communication. *Environmental Politics*, 24(1), 1–16, 2015.

B. Norheim and J. Haga, *The Three Fears Every Leader Has to Know*,
https://doi.org/10.1007/978-3-031-08984-8

Enos, Richard Leo, & Thompson, Roger, et al. (eds.): *The Rhetoric of St. Augustine of Hippo. De Doctrina Christiana & the Search for a Distinctly Christian Rhetoric*. Waco: Baylor University Press, 2008.

Fafner, Jørgen: *Tanke og tale. Den retoriske tradition i Vesteuropa*. Copenhagen: C. A. Reitzel, 1978.

Farnsworth, Ward: *Farnsworth's Classical English Rhetoric*. Jaffrey: David R. Godine, 2011.

Göpel, Maja: *How a New Economic Paradigm and Sustainability Transformations Go Hand in Hand*. Berlin: Wuppertal Institute, 2016.

Hankiss, Elemér: *Fears and Symbols*. Budapest: Central European University Press, 2001.

Harrell, Erika: "Violent victimization committed by strangers, 1993–2010." Published by U.S. Department of Justice, Office of Justice Programs, Bureau of Justice Statistics, December 2012: https://www.bjs.gov/content/pub/pdf/vvcs9310.pdf.

Heifetz, Ronald A.: *Leadership without Easy Answers*. Cambridge, MA: Belknap Press of Harvard University Press, 1994.

Hobbes, Thomas: *Leviathan*. Minneapolis: Learner Publishing Group, 2018. First published in 1651.

Hulme, M.: *Why We Disagree about Climate Change: Understanding Controversy, Inaction and Opportunity*. Cambridge University Press, 2009.

Humes, James C.: *The Sir Winston Method. Five Secrets of Speaking the Language of Leadership*. New York: William Morrow & Company, 1991.

Jaeger, Werner: *Paideia: The Ideals of Greek Culture: Vol I Archaic Greece The Mind of Athens*. Oxford: Oxford University Press, 1967.

Kennedy, George: *The Art of Rhetoric in the Roman World 300 B.C.–A.D. 300*. Eugene, Oregon: Wipf and Stock, 2008.

Kennedy, George: *Classical Rhetoric and its Christian and Secular Tradition from Ancient to Modern Times*. Chapel Hill: University of North Carolina Press, 1999.

Kierkegaard, Søren: *The Concept of Anxiety* (Transl. by Alastair Hannay). New York: Liveright Publishing Corporation, 2014.

Kimmel, Eric A.: *King Midas and Other Greek Myths*. Simon Schuster Children, 2016.

Kjeldsen, Jens E.: *Hva er retorikk?* Oslo: Universitetsforlaget, 2014.

Kuhn, Thomas S. *The Structure of Scientific Revolutions* (3rd edition). Chicago: University of Chicago Press, 1996.

Lancaster, Simon: *Winning Minds: Secrets From The Language of Leadership*. London: Palgrave Macmillan, 2015.

Latour, Bruno: *Down to Earth: Politics in the New Climatic Regime*. Cambridge: Polity Press, 2018.

Lausberg, Heinrich, et al. (ed.): *Handbook of Literary Rhetoric: A Foundation of Literary Study*. Leiden: Brill, 2002.

Locke, John: *Two Treatises of Government*. London: Everyman, 1997. First published in 1661–1664.

Machiavelli, Niccolò: *The Prince*. Charleston: Biblolife, 2008.

Mack, Peter: *A History of Renaissance Rhetoric 1380–1620*. Oxford: Oxford University Press, 2011.

Maslow, Abraham: "A Theory of Human Motivation." In *Psychological Review*, 50(4), 370–396, 1943.

Miller, William Ian: *The Mystery of Courage*. Cambridge, MA: Harvard University Press, 2002.

Misiunas, Romuald J., & Taagepera, Rein: *The Baltic States: Years of Dependence 1940–1990* (expanded edition). Berkeley and Los Angeles: University of California Press, 1993.

Moser, S. C., & Dilling, L.: *Creating a Climate for Change: Communicating Climate Change and Facilitating Social Change*. Cambridge University Press, 2007.

Müller, Gerhard; Balz, Horst, & Krause, Gerhard (eds.): *Theologische Realenzyklopädie* (36 volumes). De Gruyter, Berlin, 1976–2004.

Norheim, Bård & Haga, Joar: *The Four Speeches. Every Leader Has to Know*. London: Palgrave Macmillan (Palgrave Pivot), 2020.

Nussbaum, Martha: *Hiding from Humanity: Disgust, Shame, and the Law*. Princeton: Princeton University Press, 2004.

Nussbaum, Martha: *The Monarchy of Fear: A Philosopher Looks at Our Political Crisis*. New York: Simon & Schuster Paperbacks, 2018.

Quintillian: *The Orator's Education. Volume V: Books 11–12* (Ed. and Transl. by Donald A. Russell). Harvard: Harvard University Press, Loeb Classical Library.

Pernot, Laurent: *Epideictic Rhetoric. Questioning the Stakes of Ancient Praise*. Austin: University of Texas Press, 2015.

Ronson, Jon: *So, you've Been Publicly Shamed*. London: Macmillan, 2015.

Ross, D. G.: *Topic-Driven Environmental Rhetoric*. Routledge, 2017.

Schweizer, Peter: *Victory: The Reagan Administration's Secret Strategy That Hastened the Collapse of the Soviet Union* New York: The Atlantic Monthly Press, 1994.

Slemrod, Joel: "Saving and the fear of nuclear war." In *The Journal of Conflict Resolution*, 30(3), 403–419, September 1986.

Stoknes, P. E. *What We Think About When We Try Not To Think About Global Warming: Toward a New Psychology of Climate Action*. Chelsea Green Publishing, 2015.

Stump, Roger W.: *The Geography of Religion: Faith, Place, and Space*. New York: Rowman & Littlefield Publishers, 2008.

Svendsen, Lars Fr H.: *Frykt*. Oslo: Universitetsforlaget, 2007.

Taleb, Nassim Nicholas: *Antifragile: Things that Gain from Disorder*. New York: Random House, 2014.

Taleb, Nassim Nicholas: *The Black Swan*. New York: Random House, 2010.

Taylor, Charles: *A Secular Age*. Cambridge, MA: The Belknap Press of Harvard University Press, 2007.

Ueding, Gert (ed.): *Historisches Wörterbuch der Rhetorik* (12 volumes). Berlin/New York: Walter de Gruyter, 2015.

United States Federal Trade Commission: *The International Petroleum Cartel*, staff report to the Federal Trade Commission submitted to the Subcommittee on Monopoly of the Select Committee on Small Business, United States Senate, Washington, U. S. Govt. Print. Off., 1952.

Vestrheim, Gjert: *Klassisk retorikk*. Oslo: Dreyers forlag, 2018.

Vickers, Brian: *In Defense of Rhetoric*. Cambridge: Clarendon Press, 1988.

Wolchik, Sharon L., & Curry, Jane Leftwich: *Central and East European Politics: From Communism to Democracy*. Lanham, MD: Rowman & Littlefield, 2018.

World Commission on Environment and Development: *Our Common Future*. Oxford: Oxford University Press, 1987.

Yukl, Gary: *Leadership in Organizations*. (8th edition). New Jersey: Pearson, 2013.

Index